2—

D0395144

ANNUS HORRIBILIS

ANNUS HORRIBILIS

365 Tales of comic Misfortune

SAM JORDISON

JOHN MURRAY

First published in Great Britain in 2007
by John Murray (Publishers)
An Hachette Livre UK company

2

A CIP catalogue record for this title is available from the
British Library

ISBN 978-0-7195-2470-7

Typeset in Monotype Sabon by
Servis Filmsetting Ltd, Manchester

Printed and bound by Clays Ltd, St Ives plc

John Murray policy is to use papers that are natural,
renewable and recyclable products and made from wood
grown in sustainable forests. The logging and manufacturing
processes are expected to conform to the environmental
regulations of the country of origin.

John Murray (Publishers)
338 Euston Road
London NW1 3BH

www.johnmurray.co.uk

To Elly, with love again and as ever

Contents

Contents

A note on truthiness . . .

As far as I know, all the stories here are true. They have all at least been reported in various newspapers, websites and history books around the world at some time or other. (Whether or not you take all that as the cast-iron test for veracity is, of course, up to you.) A few were even told to me by people who claim to have witnessed them or to have been the victims/perpetrators themselves . . . (Again, up to you.)

I should also probably admit here that not all the dates are absolutely 100 per cent certain. History is surprisingly casual when it comes to recording on what day events occurred . . . Where there has been doubt, I've exercised a certain amount of authorial discretion and made (ahem!) educated guesses.

Introduction

If you think you're unlucky, compare yourself to the belly dancer whose buttock was accidentally removed by a plastic surgeon (14 March).

If you think you do foolish things, think about the man who decided that tying hundreds of helium balloons to his garden chair and taking off into the flight path of a California airport might be a fun way to spend his afternoon (2 July).

If you think you're having a bad day, contrast it with that of the jail chief who watched his prisoners escape over a fence using a trampoline he had given them (9 February).

One of the great things about life is that – no matter how bad things get – there's generally someone worse off than you. Someone whose misfortune makes you look like the happiest person on earth. Strangely, however, until now these karmic heroes have never been given the praise they deserve. *Annus Horribilis* is the book that should set the record straight.

At the moment history is written by the victors, and that's why it's so dull. What we are told about the past is little more than a long list of unusual triumphs and luck, and consequently it has very little to do with the lives that most of us lead.

After all, how can we empathize with Julius Caesar when there's no possibility of us ever commanding Roman legions, let alone having naked barbarians kneeling at our feet? What does Sir Francis Drake's glorious voyage around the world have to do with my life when I can't even afford a rowing boat? Why should you admire the building projects of the pharaohs when you're struggling to pay the mortgage on a two-bedroom home?

We can't all come top of the class. We can't all be in bands as big as The Beatles. We can't all win the Nobel Prize. We do, however, all have boundless potential for mucking stuff up, tripping over our own feet and receiving a smack around the chops from malign fate.

The huge number of failures and missed chances that make the world work never receive anything like the amount of attention grabbed by the greedy – and far more boring – minority of success stories. *Annus Horribilis* aims to redress this imbalance. It demonstrates the wonderful democracy of misfortune. It provides a healthful antidote to this age of relentlessly positive spin. It's also a good excuse for a whole bunch of funny stories about people so hopeless they should make us all feel far better in comparison.

Sam Jordison, 2007

January

1 January

2003

Residents of Tauranga in New Zealand were surprised to see a man bringing in the New Year by careering down their road at 50 m.p.h. on the back of a motorized bar stool. The oddness of the scene was only increased by the fact that the man, John Sullivan, was also half-naked and had smoke coming out of his backside. This latter phenomenon came thanks to the newspaper he had rolled up, wedged between his buttocks and set alight.

Sullivan later confessed in court to having 'had a few' and admitted that a public road wasn't the best place for a high-speed bar stool. Even so, he thought his sentence of 200 hours' community service harsh – not least, he said, because the policemen who arrested him had been 'laughing their heads off'.

2006

US President George W. Bush made his first public gaffe of the year in record time. 'As you can possibly see,' he said, 'I have an injury myself – not here at the hospital, but in combat with a cedar. I eventually won. The cedar gave me a little scratch.' These remarks were considered injudicious, considering his audience was a gathering of wounded veterans from the amputee care centre in a military hospital.

1962

Mike Smith, now probably best known to history as 'The Man Who Turned Down The Beatles', turned down The Beatles. The young band performed their first audition for him at Decca Records in London. The disappointed John, Paul, George and Ringo were told that 'groups of guitars are on the way out'. Smith also auditioned Brian Poole & The Tremeloes the same day. He signed them. The Beatles went on to have a number of hit records and are widely regarded as the biggest and best band of all time. The Tremeloes didn't and aren't.

1915

The Watchtower Tract and Bible Society of New York (aka the Jehovah's Witnesses) was today proven to be wrong in its prediction that the world would end in 1914. On the first days of January 1919, 1921, 1926, 1941, 1955 and 1976 similar predictions about the End Times coming in the immediately preceding years were equally conclusively refuted. Nineteen twenty-six was an especially disappointing New Year for the Witnesses because in the previous few years they had invested an awful lot of money in a California mansion where they intended to house the Old Testament prophets Abraham, Moses, David and Samuel, who they also thought had been due to return to earth in 1925. Naturally, they didn't.

2 January

1669

Henry Morgan was one of the most successful pirates in history. During his life he was the scourge of the Spanish and ran countless successful and highly profitable raids on their possessions in the New World. Most impressively, and unlike most of his piratical cousins, he even managed to survive until comparative old age and die of more or less natural causes (liver failure related to his constant carousing and heavy drinking).

He's also had considerable posthumous success. Since his death the jolly old sea dog has been immortalized as the 'Captain Morgan' whose name appears on thousands of rum bottles throughout the world, and has even been referenced as the author of the 'pirates' code' in the popular *Pirates of the Caribbean* films.

Things didn't always go Morgan's way, however. The most notable instance of dismal luck fell on him – and his ship, the *Oxford* – on this day in 1669. The *Oxford* was Morgan's pride and joy, the biggest in his fleet and the one on which he kept most of his treasure, including his world-renowned collection of jewels, piles of gold and silver and (appropriately enough for a pirate) more than 200,000 pieces of eight.

So it was an especially bad idea to decide to celebrate the capture of two French boats by ordering a pig to be barbecued on deck. Sparks from the grill shot off into the nearby powder-hold and set off a huge explosion, which blew off the whole of the front of the ship and sank it along with all its treasure. The blast also propelled Morgan backwards through the window of his cabin and dumped him unceremoniously in the sea.

3 January

2006

Every winter artist Trevor Corneliusen used to make a pilgrimage to the notoriously harsh desert landscape of Death Valley in California. There he pitched his tent in isolated old mineshafts and spent his time painting and meditating.

On this Tuesday in 2006 he was working on a spiritually influenced piece, consisting of a pair of ankles bound together with chains and a padlock. He'd brought along a thick length of chain and a tough Master Lock padlock so that he could model the uncomfortable position himself while he painted. It was only when he was most of the way through his drawing that he realized the crucial detail he had forgotten: to bring a key for the lock. His mother later explained that he was quite often 'absent-minded'.

The young artist had no choice but to hop to the nearest town to get help, a distance of five miles, in the hot sun across rocky and sandy terrain. He used an old miner's stick to help him on his way, but even so it was more than twelve hours before he arrived, exhausted, at a petrol station.

Ryan Ford, the local sheriff's deputy, was called to the scene, and the struggling artist managed to convince him that he was not an escapee from a chain gang by showing him the sketch he'd been trying to make of his bound feet. Paramedics were called, and after three attempts they managed to loosen his chains.

Deputy Ford also offered a penetrating criticism of the art that the young man had suffered so much for: 'It was a pretty good depiction of how a chain would look wrapped around your legs', he said.

4 January

1993

When it was discovered that its judges had chosen to hang a picture painted by a four-year-old, the annual show of the Manchester Academy of Fine Arts suffered a blow to its considerable reputation.

Young Carly Johnson's mother had entered her daughter's picture *Rhythm of the trees* as a joke, but it beat off competition from more than 800 other entrants to the exhibition. The judges, not knowing the age of its creator, had commended it for its 'certain quality of colour balance, composition and technical skill'.

Young Ms Johnson herself was less complimentary towards the rest of the prestigious show. It was, she said, 'a bit boring'.

5 January

1996

Singer Richard Versalle died when he fell on to the stage of the Metropolitan Opera House in New York from a 10-foot ladder after suffering a heart attack. He had been alone on stage, singing a section from the first scene of *The Makropulos Case*. This is an opera by Leos Janacek about the secret of eternal life. This already cruel irony was only compounded by the fact that the last line he sang was 'Too bad you can only live so long'.

6 January

2003

Viewers of the US Army-produced *Army Newswatch* in the conservative town of Webster, New York, were tonight surprised when their programme was interrupted with 20 minutes of hardcore gay pornography. Officials at the local cable TV network confessed that they were baffled about how the naughty film had come to appear on viewers' screens. Looking on the bright side, however, they did note that many complainants at least commented that the programme had maintained a military theme, although it was about the wartime German rather than the modern US army.

7 January

2004

When a customer pulled up to make an order at his local drive-through Burger King restaurant in Troy, Michigan, he was surprised to hear a speaker telling him, 'You don't need a couple of whoppers. You are too fat, pull ahead.'

Others, meanwhile, when they asked for a drink of Coke, were informed that the fast-food outlet didn't stock any. 'In fact,' came the message, 'we don't have anything. Pull ahead.'

For a good part of the day customers suffered similar abuse and insults from teenage hackers who had hidden near by and taken over the short-wave radio frequency that controlled the speakers the restaurant used to take orders.

Eventually policeman Gerry Schelinck and his deputies arrived on the scene to see if they could solve the problem. 'There's nothing you or the police can do about this,' boomed the tannoy when the lawman approached, 'so get your fat ass back inside and take your goons with you.'

8 January

1915

Back in 1915 the USS *Wyoming* was one of the finest ships in the US Navy. Indeed, so great was the boat's international reputation that it came as no surprise to its captain when Queen Marie of Romania ordered her consul-general to make the most of its brief anchorage in New York to go and pay respects on her behalf.

The captain even prepared a little ceremony for the moment when Lieutenant Commander Ethan Allen Weinberg, a charming gentleman dressed in a blue uniform with gold braid, arrived at the harbour side. Having been told that Weinberg was a former military man himself, the assiduous captain also allowed his distinguished guest to carry out an inspection of the sailors standing to attention before him.

Weinberg reprimanded some sailors for having less than perfectly clean uniforms and one or two of them for not having the correct stance, but he did it all in such a charming way that he made a thoroughly good impression.

Even more endearing to the boat's officers was the fact that Weinberg then offered to throw a lavish dinner party for them at the Astor Hotel in Times Square, telling them that they could order whatever they liked and that the bill would be directed to the Romanian embassy in Washington D.C.

By all accounts, the meal got off to a splendid start, but it was ruined half-way through, when two FBI detectives turned up to arrest Weinberg and dragged him from the dining-room. They had read an announcement of the event in the *New York Times* and realized that instead of Lieutenant Commander Ethan Allen Weinberg, the host was in reality Stanley Weyman, a well-known conman and serial impostor. Far from being the consul-general of Romania, he was actually a low-level clerk from Brooklyn. 'You could at least have waited until dessert', complained Weyman as he was being led away.

The captain of the USS *Wyoming* was equally ambivalent about the arrest. 'All I can say,' he said when reporters asked him to comment afterwards, 'is that the little guy gave one hell of a tour of inspection.'

1687

While conducting a Te Deum in honour of the recent recovery of his patron King Louis XIV from illness, French composer Jean-Baptiste Lully stabbed himself in the foot with the staff he used to keep time. Gangrene set in, and he died ten weeks later.

9 January

2007

It's always annoying when you can't find any clean underpants, but, even so, Serbian man Ivo Jerbic's response to the situation could be considered a trifle extreme. He grabbed all the old clothes in his cupboard, took them out into his garden and set fire to them, having, as he explained to local police, 'flipped out'. Subsequent events did nothing to lessen Mr Jebic's considerable anger. The wind carried the flames from his clothes to his house, and it burned to the ground.

1982

Mark Thatcher, son of British Prime Minister Margaret, got lost in the Sahara desert during the Paris–Dakar rally.

10 January

1990

To celebrate Martin Luther King Day the admirable staff of San Jose Public Library decided to make a 30-foot-high banner with the word 'Welcome' written in many different languages. It took over three months to finish, and the erection of the huge sign should have been a matter of considerable pride . . . except for one thing. A sharp-eyed Filipino security guard at the library had noticed a problem with the phrase in his language, Tagalog. Instead of saying 'Tuloy po kayo', the sign read, 'Tuli po kayo'. Not much difference in the lettering, but a huge difference in meaning. Rather than informing members of the Filipino community that they were 'welcome', the sign told them, 'You are circumcised'.

The sign was so big that four people were required to take it down.

11 January

2002

Officials in Georgetown, Texas, unwrapped the plaque they had commissioned to celebrate the fact that the actor James Earl Jones was going to speak in their town for the annual Martin Luther King holiday in four days' time. They were horrified to discover that the plaque read, 'Thank you James Earl Ray for keeping the dream alive' – a very serious mistake considering that James Earl Ray was the name of the man who shot the great civil rights leader in 1968.

1994

On his first diplomatic visit to Europe Bill Clinton's attempt to break the ice with Helmut Kohl did not go down as well as he might have hoped. 'I was thinking of you last night, Helmut, because I watched the sumo wrestling on television', the US President told the portly German chancellor.

12 January

2000

Eighty-year-old Fred Harrop's friends were surprised when, instead of delivering *Cinderella and Company: Backstage at the Opera with Cecilia Bartoli* (the book they had ordered for his birthday), Amazon sent him a volume entitled *Literate Smut*. Then they were shocked when they complained to the company and a spokesman told them, 'Well, if you think Mr Harrop is disappointed, imagine how the guy who got the opera book feels'.

13 January

2001

Daniel Everett wanted to give his girlfriend something nice. A surprise. So he took himself down to the nearest photocopying machine, pulled down his trousers and made two copies of his rear end.

Unfortunately for the 35-year-old Mr Everett, the nearest photocopier was in the St Louis County, Missouri, courthouse, and just as he was making his third copy, security stepped in and arrested him.

'What did I do? What did I do?' asked Mr Everett as the guards dragged him down from his perch. Realization dawned as the cuffs were slapped on. 'I guess you're going to arrest me', he correctly surmised. He was charged with disturbing the peace and indecent conduct. The two photocopies he had made were seized as evidence, but sadly for Mr Everett even they had not turned out as planned. The local police chief described the image as 'a big black blob', the only discernible detail being the label from Mr Everett's trousers.

14 January

2007

A TV programme investigating the 'ten most valuable treasures' from China's private collections rendered one of those 'treasures' almost worthless when it was smashed into tiny pieces on the set. The 2,500-year-old mirror, worth £500,000, was being shown to a live studio audience by a model when it fell from her hands and hit the floor.

The accident left the audience silent and stunned – none more so than the mirror's owner, Lu Fengui, who was sitting in the front row. 'The mirror has been part of my collection for sixteen years', said the distraught collector, 'and is – was – the best one out of more than a thousand mirrors.'

Superstitious pundits were especially horrified to realize that the model's seven years of bad luck only started *after* she broke the mirror.

1957

The actor Humphrey Bogart died. 'I should never have switched from Scotch to Martinis', were his last words and his final judgement on earth.

15 January

2007

Three thieves from New York broke into a shop and stole what they thought were mobile phones. Actually, they turned out to be global positioning systems, which led police straight to the culprits' house, where master criminal Kurt Husfelt was caught with his ill-gotten gains still in his hands.

1982

Mark Thatcher, previously lost on the Paris–Dakar rally, was found again.

1797

London hat maker James Hetherington today proudly wore his new invention – the top hat – and was immediately arrested. He was thrown in jail and fined £50 because he 'appeared on the public highway wearing upon his head a tall structure of shining lustre and calculated to disturb timid people'.

16 January

1996

Julius Maada Bio overthrew the government of Sierra Leone in a military coup. The first act of his short-lived and unpopular government was to call off the forthcoming elections in the African country. One of the more unusual side-effects of this action was the cancellation of a British Council-sponsored seminar at which Julius Maada Bio was to have been the star speaker. The subject? 'How Can Democracy Be Sustained?'

17 January

2007

So ardent was a Buenos Aires teenager's devotion to his local football team the Boca Juniors that he decided to get a tattoo of the club crest drawn on his back. Sadly the young fan (whose name was not released for legal reasons) was not sufficiently careful in his selection of a tattoo artist.

A police spokesman later explained the course of events: 'The tattooist supports Boca Juniors' rival, River Plate, so he got annoyed when the teenager asked him to tattoo Boca's symbol and decided to tattoo a penis instead.'

The unlucky victim remained unaware of the large cartoon todger that was permanently engraved in his skin, because there was no mirror in the parlour. So he paid up, left and went home full of pride to show off his new body art to his parents. It was they who alerted him to his misfortune.

18 January

1999

'I'm the luckiest guy in the world. The Lord is on my side.' So said Marion Barry, the mayor of Washington D.C., moments before FBI agents proved him wrong by storming into the hotel room where he was being secretly videoed smoking crack cocaine.

This was not the best quote of Barry's long and colourful career, however. Arguably, that came a few moments after his arrest (all of which was also recorded on the hidden video cameras), when he realized that the woman who had passed him the crack pipe was a police informant. 'Well, I'll be goddamned', he said, correctly noting his sudden change in fortune. 'The goddamn bitch set me up.'

Some commentators, however, prefer the statement he made after the arrest to explain the strange circumstances in which he had been discovered: 'There are two kinds of truth. There are real truths, and there are made-up truths.'

19 January

2007

Jim Burley led a long and eventually successful campaign for his local council to open a road bypass around his small village in Northumberland in order to improve safety. The £9 million road was eventually built, and just before it neared completion Burley went for a drive on one of the first sections to be opened. Within minutes he was involved in a head-on collision with a van.

Burley survived the accident, although its very occurrence did make his campaign for the bypass (which had been largely waged on grounds of safety) seem rather pointless. When reporters pointed this out to him, he told them, from between gritted teeth, that he could 'certainly see the irony in being involved in the first accident on a bypass for which I have been campaigning for twenty to thirty years'.

20 January

1982

Ozzy Osbourne surprised his fans – not to mention himself – when he bit off the head of a live bat on-stage. Ozzy had thought it was one of his rubber fakes. A full course of rabies injections followed.

21 January

1793

The assessment made by French king Louis XVI that 'the French people are incapable of regicide' was shown to be considerably wide of the mark when they chopped his head off.

22 January

1993

Wilfred Genus nearly avoided his fifteen-day sentence for carrying a concealed weapon when his friend Albert Flowers agreed to serve it for him. Flowers showed up in his friend's place at the start of the sentence at the low-security prison in Los Angeles claiming to be Genus, and they duly locked him up. Bizarre as it seems, the pair might have got away with it too, if Genus hadn't decided to make the most of his freedom by visiting a friend of his – who was in the very jail that he was supposed to be serving his time in.

When he appeared at the jail carrying cocaine and a gun, he was promptly arrested again. The inevitable consequence of this was that policemen were alerted to the fact that he was not where he should have been. Genus now found himself facing a ten-year sentence.

23 January

2006

When temperatures in the Central Asian country of Uzbekistan plummeted below −20° C, a local textile company started doing a roaring trade in fur lined underwear . . . until today, that is, when the country's infamously dictatorial government stepped in and banned the sexy slips. They said that they wanted to protect their citizens from the 'unbridled fantasies' that wearing the soft fabric might have aroused.

1978

Terry Kath, the lead singer of the rock band Chicago, was playing with a gun. He pointed it at his head and told concerned friends, 'Don't worry, it's not loaded'. They were his last words as the – loaded – gun accidentally discharged seconds later.

24 January

1999

Many thieves wear hats or hoods to conceal their identity, especially from the all-seeing eyes of security cameras. James Newsome only had a limited grasp of this principle, however. He wore an orange hard hat when he robbed a convenience store in Fort Smith, Arkansas, but, unfortunately for him, it had his name printed on the front. The woman behind the counter was even able to spell it out to police. He was quickly arrested.

'Could he have been smarter about the way he tried to cover things up? Yes, he could have', said Deputy Prosecuting Attorney Stacey Slaughter in her closing statement at Newsome's trial.

AD 41

'I am still alive!' shouted Roman Emperor Gaius Caligula after suffering no fewer than thirty knife wounds at the hands of his own guards. Then he died.

25 January

2000

Ronald Dean Cherry thought he could win some money from his local casino in Mississippi without even visiting the building. He phoned Treasure Bay Casino and told staff there that armed men would turn up and start shooting out the gaming halls if $100,000 wasn't delivered to his house within two hours. To facilitate that delivery he then told them the address of said domicile. The rest is easily guessed.

26 January

2004

Residents of Tainan City in Taiwan were surprised on this day in 2004, when whale fat and stinking blubber began to rain down on them. The whale in question was an old bull sperm whale that had been washed up dead on a beach in the south-west of the island. It weighed 50 tons and was 17 metres long. It was such a fine specimen, in fact, that the authorities decided to transport it to a university in Tainan for a post-mortem examination.

Because of the whale's immense size, it took thirteen hours, three large lifting cranes and fifty workers to get it loaded on the trailer truck for its final trip. Unfortunately, experts forgot to take into account the build-up of gas that would occur in the huge leviathan's stomach as it decayed. And so it was that, as the truck turned into a busy residential street, the beast exploded. Blood, blubber and whale entrails were blasted out of the wrecked sides of the truck, covering shop-fronts, cars and, worst of all, dozens of bystanders.

'What a stinking mess! This blood and other stuff that blew out on the road is disgusting, and the smell is really awful', a disturbed local resident told the BBC.

1785

Benjamin Franklin wrote a letter to his daughter expressing disappointment over the selection of the eagle as the symbol of the United States. He had wanted the turkey.

27 January

1699

Czar Peter the Great of Russia arrived in England on an unofficial visit. He spent his time talking to shipbuilders, imbibing as much culture as possible and even more pepper brandy. For much of the duration he stayed in the house of the famous writer and gardener John Evelyn, whose house was conveniently situated close to the famous dockyards in Deptford and was reputed to have some of the most remarkable grounds in the country – grounds that Evelyn had spent a full forty-five years laying out.

Evelyn's servant was most disturbed by the royal visitor and wrote to his master that the house was 'full of people right nasty. The Czar lies next your library, and dines in the parlour next your study. He dines at ten o'clock, and six at night; is very often at home a whole day; very often in the King's yard, or by water, dressed in several dresses . . .'

Worse still, the Czar dedicated a significant amount of his time to breaking windows, burning chairs and throwing knives at Evelyn's pictures. He and his retinue made such a mess of Evelyn's precious garden that the servant observed it 'looked as if a regiment of soldiers in iron shoes had drilled upon it'. The Czar's favourite game, meanwhile, appeared to be driving his friends into Evelyn's topiary as they sat in a wheelbarrow.

1992

Clinton Richard Doan's last action on earth was to open the door of his fridge in Ketchum, Idaho. Immediately after he did so, the beer keg he had been looking for ruptured, shot out of the fridge and hit him on the head.

28 January

1995

Twenty-one-year-old Michael Marcum was arrested for stealing six 300-plus-pound transformers from a power company substation in his home town of Stanberry, Missouri. The reason he took them? He wanted to build a time machine, so that he could go a few days into the future to find out winning lottery numbers, then return and buy a ticket.

29 January

1995

Sub-stations were causing trouble again on the very day after Michael Marcum's encounter. This time the problem was a cobra haunting the grounds of one in Tilehurst, Berkshire. An alarmed resident spotted the snake, motionless, in the upright 'attack' position. This good citizen spent a large part of a cold afternoon warning passers-by not to get too close while he looked for help. He also called the RSPCA, but they had no inspectors available in the area. So he phoned the Ark Animal Sanctuary in Caversham, who told him that the snake was probably so still because of the cold weather and that their man would be along shortly to pick it up.

Eventually Bob Andrews arrived from the sanctuary, kitted out with a box, heavy gloves and goggles to protect his eyes from the venomous animal. He stealthily and steadily made his way towards the unmoving reptile, stopping only when he realized that it was actually an old exhaust pipe. Sadly, posterity has not recorded what he said on making this discovery.

30 January

2005

A Sunday league soccer match between Peterborough North End and Royal Mail AYL had to be abandoned when the referee sent himself off. The 39-year-old Andy Wain explained: 'I heard the keeper say "It's always the bloody same with you, ref – we never get anything". It was the last straw . . .'.

Witnesses said the referee then threw down his whistle, untucked his shirt and charged up to the keeper, eyeballing him with brooding intent. 'Then', said Wain, 'I came to my senses.'

He ran back, retrieved his red card and showed it to himself, declaring his earlier actions 'totally unprofessional. If a player did that, I would send him off. So I had to go.'

2001

Eight-year-old Christopher Kissinger was suspended from his school in Jonesboro, Arkansas, under its 'zero tolerance for weapons' policy. His crime? Pointing a chicken finger at a teacher and saying, 'Pow! Pow!'

𝔷𝟙 𝓙𝓪𝓷𝓾𝓪𝓻𝔂

1991

John Kerry, the US senator and 2004 US Presidential challenger, sent the following communication to a constituent: 'Thank you for contacting me to express your support for the actions of President Bush in response to the Iraqi invasion of Kuwait. From the outset of the invasions, I have strongly and unequivocally supported President Bush's response to the crises and the policy goals he has established with our military deployment in the Persian Gulf.'

That message wouldn't have been a problem, if only he hadn't sent the exact same person the following letter only nine days earlier: 'Thank you for contacting me to express your opposition . . . to the early use of military force by the US against Iraq. I share your concerns. On January 11, I voted in favour of a resolution that would have insisted that economic sanctions be given more time to work and against a resolution giving the president the immediate authority to go to war.'

2002

A Massachusetts student bit into a turkey and tomato sandwich in her high school cafeteria and spat out part of a severed human thumb. The offending digit had belonged to a worker who had accidentally cut it off in a vegetable slicer. Another student complained not unreasonably, 'Our lunch is our most valuable time, and now we have to eat fingers'.

February

1 February

1994

Sitting in a television studio in Ohio, preparing to give a response to Bill Clinton's 1994 State of the Union address, American Republican politician Martin Hoke liked the look of the producer who attached his microphone. 'She has ze bigga breasts', he enthusiastically told his debating partner in a high-pitched Mexican accent. He followed the line with a big salacious grin – a grin that quickly froze on his face when he realized that the microphone had been switched on and that the entire globe would therefore shortly be hearing his comments.

'Well, Dad, that was a really dumb thing to say', commented Hoke's fifteen-year-old daughter Elizabeth when every American news channel and dozens of papers around the world followed up on the story.

The man himself was contrite and apologetic. 'I deserve to get a 2-by-4 to the head', he said, not without justification. A few days later his very public penance even appeared to be going well until he confided in a local news reporter that he was glad that an escaped murderer who went on a killing spree had knocked him off the front pages.

1524

In June 1523 astrologers in London had predicted that the end of the world would begin with a huge deluge of rain on 1 February 1524. Twenty thousand people are said to have left their homes, while the Prior of St Bartholemew's built a fortress where he set himself up with enough food for two months. They were all confused – and then not a little put out – when the skies remained dry.

2 February

2007

When Christopher Gay heard that his mother was dying, he was determined to go and visit her. Nothing was going to stop him – not even the fact that he was in prison in Texas and she was more than 500 miles away in Tennessee.

His adventures began in late January 2007, when he was being transported to Alabama, where he was due to stand trial for stealing several cars and trucks (a habit that was going to have considerable bearing on later events).

Gay made his getaway after he requested a lavatory stop just before Georgia. Once the cuffs were off, so was he, speeding down the highway in a stolen pick-up truck, leaving his guards in a cloud of dust.

Annoyingly for Gay, however, after just 50 miles the truck broke down. No matter. He quickly swapped it for a tractor-trailer, which got him across the border into Tennessee before it too chugged out. The resourceful Gay next managed to make off with a delivery truck from a Wal-Mart store and, having driven through most of the night, got to within 50 miles of his mother's house. Then disaster struck. He fell asleep at the wheel, and his ride careered off the road, just as a police patrol car was passing.

Terrified, Gay ran off though a thick wood and emerged 4 miles later in the car park of a Nashville night-club. There he stole the first vehicle he came across – which happened to be the tour bus of the Grammy award-winning country singer Crystal Gayle. Gay, whose tragic journey might well have been the subject of one of Gayle's songs, was now the subject of a massive manhunt.

'I could fib to you and say we finally tracked down young Mr Gay using good old-fashioned police footwork and investigation', said Jeff Hoffman, the man who eventually arrested him. 'But I'm afraid it was a bit more Keystone Kops than that. To be honest, I was driving home on Friday evening when Ms Gayle's bus passed right by me.'

Gay had passed Hoffman in the distinctive-looking bus on the road down to Daytona in Florida late at night on 2 February. Hoffman had initially been suspicious enough to pull him over, but he bought the excuse that he was on his way to the speedway because he was working for the racing driver Tony Stewart. It was only when he radioed base and discovered just which bus he'd just let go that the chase was on. Hoffman picked up his quarry just outside the track. 'He wasn't violent and he wasn't weird', he said. 'In fact, he apologized for lying earlier.'

Gay's ailing mother endorsed this positive assessment. 'I know Christopher has stolen a few things in the past,' she told reporters, 'but he has a good heart. This isn't the first time he has given his guards the slip, though. Seven years ago he escaped from jail just the same way. That time it was to see his granddaddy Joe. That's how much his family mean to him.'

Even Crystal Gayle was sympathetic, in spite of the annoyance of losing her vehicle. 'I would have lent him the bus if he had told me his story and asked me', she said, 'if it wasn't for the fact that he was breaking the law by escaping from prison.'

3 February

2004

A Brazilian football referee found himself facing life without his wife when he pulled out a pair of frilly knickers instead of a red card during a match.

The unfortunate Carlos Jose Figueira Ferro had intended to send a player off after a foul during an amateur match in Anama, but when he realized that he'd whipped out a pair of undies instead of a card, it was he who fled the field in embarrassment and horror. The game was consequently brought to a standstill twenty minutes early and, although Ferro insisted that he had never seen the knickers before, his wife, who had been watching the game, initiated divorce proceedings.

4 February

1992

Twelve years earlier than Carlos Ferro (see 3 February), but almost to the very day, Stan Guffey was also flying the flag for refereeing incompetence at a basketball match. At least, that's what Oklahoma police officer Eldridge Wyatt thought. He was so incensed at Guffey's failure to chasten a player for elbowing another that he marched on to the court and arrested him. The match was held up for ten minutes as officials tried to persuade Wyatt to let the matter drop. When the game had finished and a local reporter asked the sporting cop about the incident, Wyatt arrested him too.

5 February

2007

It was today reported that Roy Dann, the landlord of the Gordon Arms in Southampton, finally snapped and banned Jeff Donovan from his pub. For the past six years Donovan had been playing songs by Mariah Carey, every day, twenty times a day, on the pub juke-box. 'To start with, we found it amusing', said Roy Dann, but eventually the constant wailing from Mariah had just got too annoying – as had Mr Donovan's retort that 'the customer is always right' whenever the landlord complained. 'I don't care what he says now,' concluded Dann, 'he's not coming back into my pub.'

2005

Welsh rugby fan Geoff Huish was sure that his team were going to get beaten by England. 'If Wales win, I'll cut off my balls', he told friends in the week leading up to the match.

Wales won 11–9. That's why, after Huish had finished listening to the match on his radio, he chopped off his testicles with a pair of wire-cutters.

'The cutters were blunt so I had to keep snipping', Huish explained to *The Sun* newspaper. 'I cut my penis as well. There was a lot of blood, but not as much as you would expect.'

The operation took an agonizing ten minutes. Then he popped his balls into a blue plastic bag and returned with them to his friend's house to show that he had done it. There he passed out. His friend quickly put the gonads into a pint of ice, but surgeons were unable to sew them back on.

6 February

2007

When a taxi driver from Lulea in central Sweden attempted to perform a good deed after seeing a car crash, it cost him dear. He allowed three of the victims to shelter from the cold in his car and then looked on aghast as emergency services destroyed the vehicle in order to 'rescue' them.

Caring cabbie Peter Andersson explained: 'They had a few cuts and bruises, and I let them shelter in my cab. They looked worse than they were. I went off to look at the wreck and when the firemen turned up, they pulled out hydraulic metal cutters and sliced the side off the cab. They said it meant they could get the people out without them having to bend too much, in case of neck injuries. They didn't realize they only had to open the door.'

To make matters worse, his insurance company disputed his £30,000 repair bill, refusing to believe his story about how the damage had come about.

7 February

1925

'If Christ does not appear to meet his 144,000 faithful shortly after midnight on February 6th or 7th, it means that my calculations, based on the Bible, must be revised', wrote Margaret Rowen, leader of the Church of Advanced Adventists, earlier in 1925. Today she presumably started revising them.

8 February

1994

At 11.30 p.m. Robert Blank was waiting for a red light to change at Toluca Lake in Los Angeles when a black Mercedes pulled up beside him. Out of the Mercedes jumped a man looking remarkably like the famous actor Jack Nicholson. Things went from strange to scary when Nicholson (for it was indeed he) shouted, 'You cut me off!' and started striding purposefully towards Blank's car.

Blank locked his car doors, which enraged Nicholson all the more. The actor went back to his Mercedes, opened the boot and extracted a two-iron golf club. Then, in a frenzy disturbingly reminiscent of his infamous axe-wielding 'Heeeeere's Johnny' scene in *The Shining*, the multiple Oscar-winner proceeded to belabour Blank's vintage car with his makeshift weapon. He severely dented the roof and smashed the front window, cutting the terrified Blank's face in the process.

Blank later successfully sued for an undisclosed sum and Nicholson apologized profusely, explaining that the pressure of a friend's recent death and playing a 'maniac' all night for the film *The Crossing Guard* had got to him. 'I was', he explained, 'out of my mind.'

1587

Mary Queen of Scots was beheaded and, incidentally, revealed to be almost hairless. When the executioner went to lift up her head by grasping hold of her long, flowing locks, the hair came up but the head didn't. She had been wearing a wig. Underneath her hair was clipped, grey and sparse.

9 February

1997

Clifton McPip, the governor of Chisbeck County Jail, Iowa, thought he was doing the right thing when he bought a group of prisoners a trampoline. 'They provided statistics to show that open-air trampolining aided the rehabilitation process', explained the well-meaning jailer. 'I was more than happy to grant their request.'

His happiness was soon punctured, however, when prisoners started to use the trampoline to propel themselves over the prison fence. Six men escaped before the guards realized what was happening. 'It all happened so quickly', recalled one of them. 'One moment they were bouncing up and down, the next – boing! Over they went. They were like six fat birds.'

Three of the prisoners remained at large for several weeks. Fortunately the amiable Governor McPip was able to put things into perspective. 'They also asked for tunnel-digging equipment for a play they were doing about miners,' he told journalists at the time, 'but I refused. I'm not a fool.'

10 February

1910

When Admiral Sir William May received a telegram from the Foreign Office in London telling him to expect a visit to the battleship *Dreadnought* from members of the Abyssinian royal family, he immediately rolled out the red carpet. He also made sure that there was a full honour guard waiting to greet the distinguished visitors when they arrived, and he set up a barrier of saluting officers to keep unruly members of the general public at bay.

Not all went smoothly for Sir William, however. Considerable embarrassment was caused by the fact that nobody had been able to find an Abyssinian flag. No one knew how to play Abyssinia's national anthem either, so the Emperor and his entourage were greeted by a band playing the anthem of Zanzibar instead.

Fortunately the royal party didn't seem to notice this lapse. They just bustled on board the boat, grinning broadly underneath their heavy beards. Occasionally, they yelled 'bunga bunga' with delight, especially when they were shown technological marvels such as electric lights.

One strange guest would only say, 'Chuck-a-choi, chuck-a-choi', and a sudden burst of rain forced the visit to be terminated early, but on the whole Sir William must have felt pleased with his day's work. Or at least, he must have until he saw a picture of the royal party printed in a newspaper several days later, underneath a story explaining that they were actually a group of young jokers from Bloomsbury in London. The man who would only say 'chuck-a-choi' was actually a woman called Virginia Stephen, and the reason they'd retreated from the rain was for fear that their make-up might run and their beards come unstuck.

'Bunga bunga' briefly became a part of the English language, and Virginia Stephen (soon to become Virginia Woolf) went on to become renowned as a writer. She even ensured that the episode was immortalized by including it in her short story 'A Society'. 'Never have I laughed so much', she wrote.

1912

'My dear fellow,' began the famous French editor Marc Humblot in a letter to Marcel Proust, 'I may perhaps be dead from the neck up, but rack my brains as I may, I can't see why a chap should need thirty pages to describe how he turns over in bed before going to sleep.' With that, Humblot rejected Proust's manuscript of *Remembrance of Things Past*. The author eventually published it himself, and it has never been out of print since.

11 February

2006

Quail-shooting in America is a notoriously easy sport. The birds are raised in a pen and released mere seconds before they are shot. Huntsmen dress in bright orange clothing to further insure against any unlikely accidents.

All of which helps explain why the world was so astounded when the US Vice-President Dick Cheney hit the 78-year-old attorney Harry Whittington in the face, neck and chest with bird shot while on a quail hunt in Texas.

Cheney, one of the masterminds behind President Bush's invasion of Iraq and an avid hunter, was supposed to be shooting at a covey of quail when the luckless Whittington got in his line of fire. The ranch's owner, Katharine Armstrong, said Whittington was about 30 yards from Cheney when the Vice-President pulled the trigger, noting that 'Mr Whittington got peppered pretty good'.

Whittington later suffered a 'minor heart attack' and atrial fibrillation thanks to a pellet that embedded itself in the outer layers of his heart. To add disfigurement to injury, doctors decided to leave several birdshot pellets in Whittington's skin rather than risk removing them. His doctor put the number of remaining pellets at 'more than I can count on the fingers of my hand, but less than 100'.

Even so, when he emerged from hospital six days later, the loyal Republican Party fundraiser Mr Whittington appeared to harbour no grudges against his Vice-President. He even apologized for getting in the way of his bullet.

'My family and I are deeply sorry for everything Vice-President Cheney and his family have had to deal with', he said. 'We hope that he will continue to come to Texas and seek the relaxation that he deserves.'

Senator Patrick J. Leahy, who was once the target of a brutal barrage of abuse from the Vice-President that ended when Cheney suggested that Leahy 'go fuck' himself, commented: 'In retrospect, it looks like I got off easy.'

2007

When James Van Iveren heard screams and cries for help coming from a neighbour's apartment, he did the decent thing. He grabbed a sword, kicked down the door and rushed in. 'Where is she?' he kept demanding while searching the building for the unhappy woman. The occupier eventually managed to show him the pornographic DVD that had been the source of the distressed female cries – and then called the police.

'Now I feel stupid', Van Iveren said.

12 February

1951

Lieutenant-Colonel Sir Walter Bromley-Davenport was a Tory MP of the old school, famed for his loud voice, military bearing and habit of shouting 'Take your hands out of your pockets' at Labour MPs when they stood up to make their début speeches. Although he himself used the same speech at every election he fought from 1945 until his retirement in 1970, he was a popular figure and never lost his Parliamentary seat.

However, his career as a Whip for the Conservative Party was cut short following a most unfortunate event. One of the jobs of the Whips in the UK Parliament is to make sure that party members attend important votes. So when Bromley-Davenport saw a smartly dressed figure exiting the House of Commons just before a crucial motion went to the vote, he was eager to persuade him to return, presuming him to be a recalcitrant Tory. The man ignored his summons, however. Thoroughly annoyed, Bromley-Davenport landed a smart kick on his posterior, sending him tumbling down a flight of steps. It was only when the man informed him that he was not a member of the Conservative Party but was in fact the Belgian ambassador that Bromley-Davenport realized his error.

2002

Carl Franklin was answering nature's call, facing a fence, fag in hand, when he was spotted by a policeman. In a mad rush to get away he pocketed the cigarette and ran for it. His progress was halted, however, when his trousers caught fire in a particularly painful place; he was forced to drop them and then tripped when they fell around his ankles.

13 February

1813

General Sir William Erskine was one of the most unusual commanders in British military history. Described as 'a near-sighted old ass' by his fellow General Harry Smith, Erskine's sanity was as unreliable as his eyes. Before he went to fight under the Duke of Wellington in the Peninsular War he had twice been committed to an asylum. After his appointment, although the British military secretary assured the famous Duke that Erskine was 'lucid at times', he also warned him that 'he did look a little mad as he embarked'.

Erskine's fitness to command was soon brought into question during the Battle of Sabrugal, when he marched his forces the wrong way. His constant need to have the whereabouts of the enemy pointed out to him before he could engage them was also a problem.

Wellington managed to control his anger, however, until the last days of the protracted siege of a fort at Almeida, when it fell upon Erskine to protect a bridge vital in preventing the French garrison from escaping.

The order arrived while Erskine was dining with a colleague. Wellington had commanded that he send some cavalry and infantry, so Erskine detached a corporal and four privates. When it was put to him that he might as well send 'a pinch of snuff' to protect such a vital position, Erskine changed his mind and decided to send a whole regiment. He wrote out the order, put the order in his pocket – and then promptly forgot about it. The bridge was lost, the French escaped and Wellington was justly furious about 'the most disgraceful military event that has yet occurred to us'.

Bad as that was, the true nadir of Erskine's career came on this day in 1813, when he ended his own life by jumping from a window in Lisbon. Shortly after hitting the ground, and shortly before breathing his last, he was heard to ask bystanders, 'Why did I do that?'

2002

A meeting held by Bath and North-east Somerset council to discuss voter apathy did not go well. Just one member of the public bothered to turn up.

14 February

2007

Therese Smith, an eighty-year-old woman from Boca Raton, Florida, made a dramatic entrance when summoned to an examination centre to retake her driving test. She drove her car right through the wall of the Deerfield Beech centre's office, injuring eleven people in the process (fortunately none of them seriously).

1779

The famous navigator James Cook, one of whose chief interests was the cannibalistic habits of islanders in the South Sea, was killed during a fracas with native Hawaiians. All that his crew were able to retrieve of his body were a few bones and pieces of salted flesh.

15 February

2001

A Norwegian motorist was today fined and sent to jail for throwing a speed camera into the sea. The camera had snapped the nineteen-year-old man driving too fast, so he'd panicked, lifted it off its ten-foot pole and thrown it over a cliff.

'It's the most stupid thing I have ever done', he admitted afterwards, his regret no doubt heightened by the fact that someone had spotted him at work on the camera and shopped him to police. For the offence he was fined a tidy £9,000 and given eighteen days in prison. Just to rub salt into the wound, it was also revealed today, at his trial, that the police had found the camera with its film intact and he was fined £250 for doing 68 m.p.h. in a 50 m.p.h. zone.

16 February

1856

Destroying your best cattle, burning your crops and stopping all work isn't generally considered the best way of guaranteeing the future health and happiness of your people, but back in 1856 the Xhosa tribe in South Africa were convinced it was going to do the trick.

They'd been so persuaded by a fourteen-year-old girl who had returned from bathing in the river one day with a strange story about several unusual-looking men who had tried to engage her in conversation. Her uncle Umhlakaza, a renowned local seer, knew straight away what was going on. These strangers were spirits. He hurried down to the river to confer with them and wasn't at all surprised to see that several of them were his dead relatives.

The ghostly beings offered him a remarkable deal. If the Xhosa people destroyed most of their means of supporting themselves, the sun would reverse direction across the sky on 18 February 1857, the fertility of their fields would be restored, grain would overflow for ever in their storehouses, countless herds of disease-free cattle would appear on the land, their rivers would flow with milk and, best of all, the hated British colonialists who threatened their borders would be swept into the sea in a tidal wave. If, however, they failed to keep their side of the bargain, they'd all be turned into little bugs and squashed.

It was clear that the Xhosa would be far better off if they honoured the deal, and Umhlakaza was able to persuade thousands and thousands of them to obey his spirit guides. Over the next few months 200,000 cattle were killed, acres of crops were burned and nearly all work stopped in the fields as people laboured instead to build new kraals for the spirit cattle and new skin sacks for the rivers of milk.

At dawn on 18 February thousands gathered to watch the sun rise. When it came up as usual, and travelled its accustomed way across the sky, the magnitude of their mistake began to dawn on them. Already disease and famine had begun to set in because of their insane gullibility, and now battles quickly broke out over the remaining food. By the end of the year as many as 50,000 people had died, and the region was firmly under the control of the British, who had stepped in to provide food for the desperate people.

Umhlakaza himself went into hiding and died of starvation. His niece survived until 1898, but if she ever met any strange men by a river again, she kept it firmly to herself.

17 February

2006

The funeral of Serbian man Bogoljub Topalovic was halted when the man himself called his daughter to ask why no one had been to visit him in hospital recently.

It was a great day for his no longer mourning family – after they had overcome the shock – but not so good for a nurse in the Novi Sad clinic where Mr Topalovic was being treated. It seems that the nurse had been tipping off a local funeral home about upcoming funerals to earn extra cash, but this time around she had wrongly informed them of the 84-year-old's death and they'd mistakenly buried another corpse from the hospital. So it was that Mr Topalovic finally got a visit, his relatives who had flown over from America went back and the nurse received a well-deserved reprimand.

18 February

2007

The author of a First World War history today found that his book had been taken off the shelves in Swindon Tourist Information

Centre. This removal had been effected, he was told, because he did not have the right insurance.

Mark Sutton's book *Tell Them of Us* went on sale in October 2006 and had sold more than a thousand copies through the Information Centre before the local council realized that it posed a health and safety risk. A spokesman explained: 'We have to cover for every eventuality – even if that is an accident caused by pages falling out of the book. Nobody is denying it's a very small risk, but the risk is there.'

Council workers told Mr Sutton that he could get the necessary £5 million cover for 'as little as £150', but he refused to stump up the cash, invoking the memory of men to whom the book was dedicated, and who had faced far greater risks than paper cuts.

1478

The Duke of Clarence, younger brother of King Edward IV of England, was drowned in a vat of malmsey wine.

19 February

2002

When they started at dawn, everything seemed to be going according to plan for the thirty British Royal Marines on an amphibious training exercise. Just as they'd been instructed, they'd left their landing craft and stormed up a beach wielding their assault rifles and mortars . . . No one fell over; everyone was present and correct.

There was soon some confusion, however. The troops had been told that, when they landed on the British Mediterranean territory of Gibraltar, other soldiers would be there to greet them, firing blanks into their path and pretending to be the enemy. Instead, all they could see was a few confused and frightened-looking fishermen. When the enemy finally did appear, there were only two of them, and they were wearing the uniform of the Spanish police force.

It was these two policemen who explained the mistake to the British unit (which incidentally – and rather fortunately – likes to list one of its major characteristics as 'cheerfulness in the face of adversity'). They had landed in Spain instead of Gibraltar, inadvertently invading the beach of San Felipe, near the town of La Linea.

The marines quickly retreated and moved on to the real Gibraltar, easily recognizable, as the locals pointed out to them, because of the 1,398 foot rock that stuck out the top of it.

A Ministry of Defence spokesman said it was a situation that he would 'rather not had taken place'. Nevertheless, he said that no one intended to take disciplinary action against the troops, who appeared to have taken a wrong turning in bad weather, stating simply, 'I am sure some lessons have been learned'.

20 February

1995

Considering that he was just about to have his left foot amputated, William King was in a remarkably good mood shortly before he underwent the anaesthetic. 'Make sure you don't take the wrong one', he joked shortly before he was wheeled into the operating theatre.

Unfortunately, the surgeon at the University Community Hospital in Tampa, Florida, did just that. When King awoke, it was to discover that his right leg had been removed below the knee, and he was going to have to undergo another operation to remove the correct leg: his gangrenous left one.

In order to prevent such undesirable occurrences happening again, the hospital implemented a space-age solution. They started writing 'no' in marker pen on limbs that were supposed to remain attached to patients' bodies.

21 February

2007

A routine operation on an appendix went awry when the surgeon left the room to have a fight. All was proceeding as normal when one Dragan Vukanic walked into the theatre, insulted the operating surgeon, Spasoje Radulovic, and, according to a witness, pulled his ear and slapped him on the face.

When Vukanic then stormed out of the room, Radulovic downed his tools and set off in hot pursuit. The two slugged it out in the corridor, furnishing each other with several bruises, split lips and a fractured finger.

Fortunately an assistant doctor was able to keep his cool and finish off the operation on the patient, who remained blissfully ignorant of the whole strange affair and made a full recovery.

2002

Donald Rumsfeld, US Defence Secretary, wanted to clear a few things up. 'I believe what I said yesterday', he said. 'I don't know what I said, er, but I know what I think . . . well, I assume it's what I said.'

22 February

1994

Austin, Texas, resident Mireya Funair's otherwise ordinary day was spoiled when a cement truck tipped over on to her car, its roof was pierced by the truck's funnel and she was buried up to her neck in concrete. It took rescuers forty minutes to free her.

23 February

2007

A woman in Romania was hospitalized with stomach cramps, saying she had swallowed a foreign object but refusing to divulge what it was. When X-rays showed that a set of false teeth were lodged in her stomach, she admitted that she had swallowed them from her husband's mouth while they were engaged in what she described as 'a special type of passionate kiss'. After two days in hospital she was able to get rid of the teeth the usual way.

24 February

2004

A man who lovingly turned his flat into a zoo for thousands of insects and creepy-crawlies saw his dream turn into a nightmare when he was bitten by his favourite black widow spider Bettina – and then eaten by his other pets.

Police were called into the flat of Mark Voegel from Dortmund, Germany, after neighbours complained about the smell. The shocked officers said it was 'like a scene from a horror movie'. They found the remains of the thirty-year-old loner draped across a sofa, covered in giant cobwebs. Voegel's pet gecko Helmut was cheerfully gorging on its former master's remains, together with over 200 spiders, more than 2,000 termites and several snakes.

'Spiders were running all over him', said a spokesman. 'They were coming out of his nose and mouth. Larger pieces of flesh had been torn off by the lizards and were taken back to the webs of tarantulas and other bird-eating spiders. There were open cages and terrariums everywhere – all bathed in a weird green light. It was horrible.'

25 February

2006

Nick Flynn, a visitor to the Fitzwilliam Museum in Cambridge, destroyed three Qing Dynasty Chinese vases worth £500,000. He claimed to have suffered a 'Norman Wisdom moment' of extreme clumsiness, tripping over his shoelaces and landing on the vases.

After the sad event he was surprisingly unrepentant. 'I was surprised that,' he told the BBC, 'seeing they were the prize possession of the museum, they were just lying on a window sill . . . I thought they might take a little bit better care of them.'

Patient museum officials pointed out that they had been in the same place unharmed for years and years before Mr Flynn came along.

26 February

1995

Barings Bank was one of the most venerable in the world. It was the private banker to the British Queen, it had helped fund the Louisiana Purchase in 1803 and it had underwritten the Napoleonic Wars. The firm had a cast-iron reputation for security and probity.

Nick Leeson, meanwhile, was one of their star traders. Aged just twenty-seven, he already headed the bank's office in Singapore, and his skill at betting on market shifts around the world at one point accounted for a full 10 per cent of the bank's total profits.

'It is not actually terribly difficult to make money in the securities markets' was the expert opinion of Peter Baring, the bank's chairman, and he and his colleagues just let Leeson get on with the fun business of making them lots of yummy money. They also let him – or, at least, failed to stop him – trade massively on the future direction of the Japanese stock market, concealing losses he made in a fraudulent account within Barings and leaving them to cover any losses he made. And when the Japanese stock market plummeted in the wake of an earthquake that hit Kobe, those losses were astronomical. The bank suddenly found itself with debts totalling £1.3 billion.

Two days before his twenty-eighth birthday, meanwhile, Leeson faxed his resignation to his employers, scribbled a quick note saying 'I'm sorry' on his desk and did a runner. Barings collapsed today, and the bank that once raised the money to buy an entire US state was sold for the princely sum of £1.

27 February

2007

Police patrolling the Israeli embassy compound in El Salvador were surprised to stumble across a figure lying prone on the ground. It was a man, clearly very drunk and in some distress, with his hands tied behind his back, wearing only bondage gear and with a rubber ball gagging his mouth.

Once the rubber ball had been removed from his mouth, the man was able to identify himself. 'I am Tzuriel Refael, Israeli ambassador to El Salvador', he told police. The funniest thing about this absurd statement was that it turned out to be true. The ambassador was recalled immediately, and a foreign ministry official told the AFP news agency that it was 'the last straw'.

'During the sixty years of the State of Israel, some of our diplomats have caused us embarrassment, as happens in every country', the official said. 'But an ambassador behaving indecently on a public thoroughfare – that has never happened before.'

28 February

2002

Prince Philip, the husband of the British Queen Elizabeth II, had a politically sensitive meeting with some Australian Aborigines, but that didn't stop him asking some pretty searching questions. 'Do you still throw spears at each other?' he wanted to know.

March

1 March

2004

After surviving a 10,000-volt electric shock in 1992, Dimitri Butakov became convinced that he was immortal. He wanted to convince others too, so twelve years later he invited journalists to a special event where he would prove his unusual gift. When a small crowd gathered at the appointed time, he drank half a litre of anti-freeze. He didn't die, so he started on a second half-litre. And promptly collapsed into a coma, from which he did not emerge.

1954

The 15-megaton hydrogen bomb Castle Bravo was launched at Bikini Atoll in the Pacific Ocean, resulting in one of the worst cases of radioactive contamination ever caused by nuclear testing. Looking on the bright side, however, this unpleasant event did at least inspire the name of a rather fetching piece of swimwear that had its public début in the same year.

2 March

2007

So delighted were the expressions on the faces of six schoolboys watching bare-breasted women go past them on motorcycles in today's 'Boobs on Bikes' parade in Christchurch, New Zealand, that a photographer just had to take their picture.

It was a nice shot too – the six boys can be seen clearly, laughing and cheering and looking very smart indeed in their school uniforms. The photograph was so good, in fact, that it appeared on the front of local paper *The Press* the following day . . . and that was when the youngsters stopped smiling. Their headmaster spotted the boys and busted them for being away from school on a Friday. The six were nearly expelled, but the headmaster later relented and downgraded their punishment to detention.

In spite of the trouble he got into, twelve-year-old James Hardy had no regrets. 'It was worth it', he told the local paper. 'It was funny as.'

3 March

2002

Forty-year-old Paul Kowley and 32-year-old Kim Fontana scooped a 2003 Darwin Award (the annual honours bestowed posthumously on people who stupidly cause their own deaths) for the impromptu – and fatal – shag they had on a Sheffield street. The couple wandered out of a pub, considerably the worse for wear, noticed that a street lamp wasn't working and that the tarmac beneath it was therefore dark – and used said asphalt for some ass-feeling.

Subsequent reports stated that the amorous couple were warned of the dangers of their unusual lovemaking position by three passing drivers. An off-duty paramedic even told them, 'You want to get up or you'll be run over'. 'Cheers, mate', Paul replied and blithely carried on getting it on.

Shortly afterwards tragedy struck. The driver of a single-decker bus mistook Paul and Kim for a bag of rubbish lying at the edge of the darkened road and, as one journalist put it, proceeded to press the couple like a pair of trousers. Paramedics found Kim lying on her back with her jumper pulled up, and Paul between her legs with his boxer shorts around his ankles. As the Darwin Award moderators pointed out, the unlucky pair did at least answer the question

Paul McCartney posed on The Beatles' *White Album*: 'Why Don't We Do It in the Road?'

4 March

2007

The mistake that pensioner Arthur Bulmer made was to ask his council for permission before he moved some sand from his garden to the beach. The sand had blown on to his property after winter storms and was, according to Mr Bulmer, of a very high quality – far nicer than the sand already on the beach, as it had been cleaned and refined by the wind and wasn't covered with dog mess. 'The sand is not my property. It has just invaded my garden from the beach over the road', he also explained.

'Dumping anything from your garden on to the beach constitutes fly-tipping under the Neighbourhoods and Environment Act', countered a council spokesman.

In UK law fly-tipping is a serious offence. If the law-abiding 79-year-old had taken it upon himself to move the offending sand, he could have faced a fine of up to £50,000, along with the confiscation of his vehicle – in this case a wheelbarrow.

When informed of this decision, the perplexed Mr Bulmer naturally resorted to the local press to try to get it reversed, providing a neat summation of the situation in the process. 'It's crazy', he said.

5 March

2007

A street cleaner parked her sweeper vehicle at a kerbside in Boulder, Colorado, and was just starting to walk away from the vehicle when she heard its engine start. She turned around and saw it disappearing up the road in as close an approximation to top speed as a sweeper can attain. Then it started doing doughnuts. Inside was Jeffery Strom, who, not surprisingly, was a little the worse for drink. After a brief, absurd, chase police officers removed Strom from the vehicle, and he explained, somewhat confusingly, that he hadn't meant to steal the vehicle – only to drive it away.

6 March

1835

Thomas Carlyle spent years slaving over the first volume of his *History of the French Revolution*. When he had finished, he proudly handed over the handwritten volume to his friend and mentor John Stuart Mill for review and commentary. Mill quickly realized that the book was a work of genius. Less sure was Mill's maid, however. She thought it was just scrap paper and today used it to start a fire.

Carlyle had to write the whole thing again, by hand.

7 March

2007

Joergen Mueller's day started off badly when he filled up his petrol car with diesel. It got even worse when, rather than pay the £200 his local garage asked to do the job, he tried to siphon out the diesel using the sucking power of his vacuum cleaner. As soon as the diesel hit the hot machinery of the vacuum, there was a dramatic explosion, accompanied by a large fireball. Several hours later Mr Mueller woke up in hospital, to the sight of a waiting policeman, eager to charge him with criminal negligence.

8 March

2007

Cocaine dealers are able to operate most effectively if the police don't know about them. That's why, with the benefit of hindsight, Bennie Rangel might have chosen not to post details of his illegal business on myspace.com. All the pictures that he placed on the famous networking website of himself fondling money probably weren't a good idea either – not least because they helped convince a judge to sentence the 26-year-old Texan to seventy years in prison.

9 March

2000

When Robert Challender of Reno, Nevada, turned up a month late to register his car, a 1978 Datsun, he expected to be hit with a fine. The bill he was given was larger than he was expecting, however. It was for $378,426.25 – an amount that included about $260,000 in late fees and penalties. 'I thought the bill was a bit steep', he later understated. 'I told them to take me to jail if they had to. I wasn't paying.'

Eventually it transpired that a computer glitch had caused him to be mistakenly charged for fees going back to 1900 – a time when there were no cars at all in Nevada, let alone 1978 Datsuns. 'We hope we don't see that again', said a spokesperson for the US Department of Motor Vehicles. 'Billing for 100 years of late fees is kind of shocking.'

10 March

1735

Edinburgh in the mid-eighteenth century was a tough town, not least because the man in charge of keeping the peace, Captain John

Porteous, was so keen on hurting and maiming everyone that crossed his path.

The most famous incidence of his unique take on the justice system occurred during a dispute over a vacancy in a city church. The two candidates to fill the position, a Mr Wotherspoon and a Mr Dawson, had received an equal number of votes in the parish election, leading to considerable controversy when Wotherspoon was eventually given the job.

Trouble was expected on the day of Wotherspoon's first sermon, and trouble came. Supporters of both sides crowded to the church, and Porteous followed hot on their heels. When he arrived, he discovered that Dawson had already gained control of the pulpit, so in order to keep the peace he started a riot.

According to the *Newgate Calendar*, Porteous first went up the steps to the pulpit 'without the least ceremony', took hold of Dawson by his collar and dragged him down 'like a thief'. Dawson died of his injuries a few weeks later.

Just after Porteous had finished beating Dawson, the unfortunate churchman's rival Mr Wotherspoon arrived – and by that time Dawson's Christian supporters were so enraged by what had just happened to their champion that they determined to even the score by setting upon Wotherspoon and beat him to death too. The net result was hours and hours of bloody fighting and the tedious need to run another parish election.

11 March

2007

Fifteen-year-old Cody Webb was today surprised to be sent to jail. All he'd done was call his school in Philadelphia to find out about timetable delays. Admittedly he'd done this at the slightly odd time of 3.15 a.m., but his punishment of twelve days in a juvenile detention centre could still be considered excessive.

Cody's problem was that an anonymous caller had rung the same line (which provided a range of school-related information to students and also contained an answering machine service for them to leave messages) almost exactly an hour after he did and left a bomb threat. School authorities were convinced they'd found the culprit when they checked the time records of incoming calls and Cody's number came up. The trouble was that they'd forgotten to take into account the fact that the clocks had just gone forward an hour for Daylight Saving Time.

Cody was summoned into the school office and faced a less than meticulous interrogation from the principal. He told local television station KDKA that she asked him his phone number and then right away 'she started waving her hands in the air and saying "we got him, we got him!" They just started flipping out, saying I made a bomb threat to the school.' Cody said that his attempt to protest his innocence fell on deaf ears, claiming that the principal said, 'Well, why should we believe you? You're a criminal. Criminals lie all the time.'

In spite of this fierce logic Cody refused to confess and so was sent straight to a juvenile detention centre, where he spent twelve days. When his case did finally get to court, it was reported that a judge took 'seconds' to dismiss it after properly looking at the phone records.

12 March

2007

When passers-by saw an old man looking thoughtful and sad on the roof of his house in the German city of Magdeburg, they feared the worst. Several contacted police, telling them they were worried that he may have been contemplating suicide.

It turned out that the 91-year-old had been taking advantage of some fine spring weather to re-tar his roof. His problem was that he slipped and became fixed to the sticky bitumen. A police spokesman said that when they arrived, he was 'like a beetle on its back', his arms and legs waving helplessly in the air, unable to free himself because of his advanced years. Happily firefighters were quickly able to remove him unhurt from the black ooze, although his clothes were completely destroyed.

13 March

1992

Racist skinhead group Violent Storm tempted fate too far on this Friday 13th, when they drove into a really violent storm on the M4 motorway near Bristol. A gust of wind lifted their vehicle six feet into the air and smashed it into a bridge.

14 March

2007

A German plastic surgeon was today ordered to pay £12,000 compensation to a German belly dancer after accidentally sucking out one of her buttocks. Julia 'Cleopatra' Meyer had wanted thinner thighs, but the surgeon somehow managed to suck out the fat from her right bum cheek instead.

'Because of the local anaesthesia I did not realize what he was doing', Meyer told the court. 'When I saw afterwards that half of my bum was missing, I almost fainted. It had been completely sucked away.'

Meyer had initially asked for £6,000, but after considering the effect the loss of her buttock would have on her career and the fact that she couldn't even go to her local swimming-pool any more because of the embarrassment, the judge awarded her twice that amount.

When asked for an expert opinion, a consultant at the Berlin Charité hospital described it, with notable accuracy, as a 'grave error in treatment'.

1883

'Go on, get out – last words are for fools who haven't said enough.' So, according to popular legend, said Karl Marx to his house-keeper, who had urged him to tell her his last words so she could record them for posterity. Then he died.

15 March

2006

Chicago police – who were chasing Jakub Fik after he'd been on a vandalism spree – were surprised when he severed his own penis and threw it at them. He was taken into custody and for restorative surgery. He later explained that he'd been upset by problems he was having with his girlfriend.

1978

Burt Reynolds today autographed his star on the Hollywood Walk of Fame. When he wrote his famous name in the cement, he spelt it wrong.

16 March

1995

Grant Shittit, a beautifully named resident of Timaru, New Zealand, had drunk so much that he needed a lie down on his way home. In the darkness he found what he decided was a lovely soft bed of 'moss' and promptly fell asleep, waking only briefly to be sick on himself.

His hangover the following morning was not made any easier by the realization that the moss he thought he had lain on was actually wet cement, and he was now stuck fast, with only his head free. He remained there for seventy-two hours, his cries for help becoming increasingly desperate, until a passing motorist mistook his head for an injured hedgehog and stopped. He was eventually freed by firemen with pneumatic drills.

17 March

1939

In 1939 the Bonwit Teller store on New York's Fifth Avenue was a renowned name in female fashion. The shop was so prestigious that they even managed to persuade Salvador Dalí to decorate one of their windows. 'Dalí sleeps best after receiving a tremendous quantity of cheques', the artist was fond of saying, and when the store offered him a sufficient quantity of money, he leaped at the chance to work for them.

So it was that on the night of 16 March, soon after the last customer had left, the dapper Catalan artist began to transform the storefront into a Surrealist tableau based on the theme of night and day.

For day, Dalí arranged a claw-footed bathtub lined with black Persian lambskin and filled with narcissi floating in muddy water. Arising from the tub were three arms holding up mirrors, and beside it stood a female mannequin in a state of severe undress. Her nudity was covered only by a few strategically placed chicken feathers, her waist-length hair crawled with bugs, and blood red tears streamed down her face.

For night, meanwhile, Dalí placed another mannequin in a different window. This one lay on a bed of glowing coals under a stuffed trophy, which the artist described as 'the decapitated head and the savage hoofs of a great somnambulist buffalo extenuated by a thousand years of sleep'. Naturally.

The whole thing was successfully completed before dawn, and Dalí returned to bed in good time for the shop to open its doors at 9.30 a.m. the following morning. Surprisingly, however, Bonwit Teller's conservative customers didn't understand – or even like – the Surrealisimo's creation. An outraged few even complained to the management about the nudity of the mannequins. Assuming that the customers must be right, shop managers decided to drape the bathing dummy in a ball gown, and they replaced the reclining beauty altogether with an ordinary sitting mannequin from within the store.

When a sleep-deprived Dalí arrived back to review his work and discovered that these 'improvements' had been made, he was outraged. He tore through the store shouting and swearing in French and Spanish, further distressing the store's refined clientele.

He made a beeline for the 'Day' display, intent on knocking over his mud-filled bathtub. The farce quickly turned into a comedy when he tripped over and fell through the window, spilling over on to Fifth Avenue in a hail of broken glass and a deluge of filthy water. He tumbled straight into the path of two passing policemen, who promptly arrested him.

1955

The famous writer Anaïs Nin married her lover, Rupert Pole. The happy day was marred only by her knowledge that she was already married, a fact she managed to avoid telling her new husband for eleven years.

18 March

2003

Workers at The Grange, a non-profit non-partisan organization that provides legal services for people in rural Washington State, were surprised on this Tuesday morning in 2003, when they arrived at their building to find a young protester blocking their way.

When they asked him what he was doing, Jody Mason, who had tied one end of a chain around his neck and the other around the door to the Grange offices, told them that he was making a stand against George Bush's foreign policy. He'd been righteously enraged by the mendacious President's latest televised ultimatum to Saddam Hussein and decided to do something about it. He was going to disrupt energy supplies, which is why, he explained, he'd chained himself to the federal Department of Energy office door.

Once they'd finished laughing, the Grange employees informed the unfortunate Mason that he'd attached himself to the wrong building. Later, local police officers used heavy-duty bolt cutters to free the young idealist.

'He asked for help because he didn't have the key', a police spokesman explained.

1584

Czar Ivan the Terrible of Russia died while in the middle of a game of chess – with himself. Right up until his last breath Ivan had refused to take on any living opponents at the game, declaring it unthinkable that anybody could defeat the czar of Russia.

19 March

2003

Coca-Cola launched its Dasani brand of water in the UK with the kind of fanfare that only a multinational on that scale can manage. A £7 million advertising campaign explained that the product was 'as pure as bottled water gets', thanks to a 'highly sophisticated purification process' based on nothing less than NASA spacecraft technology.

The expensive launch quickly began to turn into a full scale PR disaster when it was revealed that the 'highly sophisticated purification process' was actually the same reverse osmosis used in many cheap domestic water-filtering products. What's more, the special 'pure' water was actually ordinary tap water. It cost Coca-Cola approximately 0.03p a litre to pump it into its factory in Kent. When it came out the other end, labelled 'pure', it cost 95p a litre: a mark-up of a healthy 3,000 per cent.

Things got worse still when it was discovered that the bottles of Dasani in the shops appeared to be contaminated with a cancer-causing chemical. During the 'purification' process Coke had pumped calcium chloride, containing bromide, into the water for 'taste profile'. When they then pumped ozone through the water, the harmless bromide oxidized and turned into bromate – a big problem.

The news broke on 19 March. All 500,000 bottles were withdrawn within twenty-four hours.

20 March

1998

Almost five years to the day before Coca-Cola had to withdraw Dasani from the UK, they were heading for another disaster in the USA. When the company had offered schools in Georgia the chance to win some money by finding the most elaborate way to celebrate 'Coke in Education', the principal of Greenbriar High School had leaped in with both feet. She and the school board decided to hold a special 'Coke Day'. All the pupils were instructed to wear Coke T-shirts, Coca-Cola company executives were invited to hold special seminars, and then, in the *pièce de resistance*, all the logo-clad pupils were going to pose for photos, arranging themselves into shapes that spelled out the company's name. For these egregious services to corporate culture, the school was to be awarded $500 and the chance to win a further $10,000 national grand prize.

All went well, until it came to photo time and one pupil, Mike Cameron, decided to assert his individual identity by revealing a Pepsi branded T-shirt.

'In my eyes, I didn't do anything wrong', the freedom-loving Cameron later explained – but by then he was serving the one-day suspension his principal had given to him for embarrassing the school in front of all the assembled dignitaries from Coca-Cola.

'I know it sounds bad – "Child suspended for wearing a Pepsi shirt on Coke Day"', said Gloria Hamilton, the school principal, but she still attempted to get the suspension included in young Cameron's permanent record. Fortunately, the subsequent media furore forced the school to wipe Cameron's slate clean, while he went on to become something of a countercultural hero – not to mention a great advert for Pepsi. A spokesman for that company commented: 'Without knowing all the details, it sounds like Mike's obviously a trendsetter with impeccable taste in clothes.'

21 March

1983

Princess Diana met a one-armed man during a royal tour of Australia. 'My, you must have fun chasing the soap around the bath!' she exclaimed tactfully.

22 March

1997

Brazilian fisherman Nathon do Nascimento choked to death when a six-inch fish jumped out of the water and down his throat during a long yawn.

23 March

1994

Aeroflot flight 593 crashed when the pilot made the elementary mistake of handing over the controls of the plane to his fifteen-year-old son, who promptly disengaged auto-pilot and accidentally set the plane into a dive from which it did not recover.

24 March

1998

Subhasinghe Premasiri, a Sri Lankan man charged with stealing gas cookers, brought a figure of speech to life today.

Angered at being accused of a crime, Premasiri turned up in

court forearmed with a bag full of faeces. When he was asked to take the witness stand, he launched the poo-filled projectile at the two policemen who had nabbed him in the first place. As it arced through the air, the bag full of shit hit a ceiling fan, became entangled and, as an official delicately put it, 'the entire court was showered with excreta'.

Premasiri was remanded by the chief magistrate for insulting the dignity of the court (which had to be cleaned before the case could continue).

25 March

1998

Early on in 1998 the residents of Garland, a peaceful suburb of Dallas, Texas, were surprised to find in their midst a group of about 150 Taiwanese people, who all wore white clothes and cowboy hats and rode about their quiet streets on bikes. It was Chen Tao, a group led by the charismatic Ho-Ming Chen. They had just bought more than thirty properties in hard cash, and they claimed that they had a spaceship.

This latter fact emerged when the group decided to hold a press conference to explain their presence to the confused local media. At the conference Chen also explained that 2,000 years ago he had fathered Jesus and now communicated with God via a very expensive diamond ring, which he wore back-to-front on his hand. Then Chen introduced the journalists to reincarnations of both Jesus Christ and the Buddha (an eleven-year-old and an eight-year-old, both from Taiwan). The climax was a tour around the group's aforementioned 'Godplane', a spaceship made from boxes and complete with a wooden deck, cinder blocks, rubber tyres, pole lanterns and a barbecue where one might have expected to find the control panel.

This 'Godplane', said to be capable of holding 100,000 people, was going to lift the repentant out of trouble when Armageddon came in 1999. The full details of how this would happen were due to be divulged at midnight on 25 March, when God was due to broadcast on Channel 18 of the local cable network.

When the appointed time for this miraculous broadcast arrived, however, Chen and his followers were surprised to find that the cable network wasn't running any programmes at all. All that they could see on the screen was snow.

The 'God programme' had been due to run until 31 March, when God would come to earth and shake hands with everybody in the world and speak to them in their own language. When this didn't appear to have happened either, Chen told another press conference of local reporters, 'Since God's appearance has not been realized, you can take what we have preached as nonsense'.

He then gave them ten minutes either to stone him to death or to crucify him as a false prophet. No one took him up on his offer, and Chen walked away unscathed but still very embarrassed.

26 March

1827

'Wine is both necessary and good for me', announced the famous composer Ludwig van Beethoven cheerily, shortly before dying from cirrhosis of the liver, aged fifty-seven.

27 March

1931

The celebrated English novelist Arnold Bennett died of typhoid contracted from drinking a glass of tap water in a Paris hotel. He drank the water to prove to companions that it was completely safe.

28 March

2002

A Chinese man's attempt to rob a house in Tokyo ran into difficulties when the building he broke into turned out to be a police dormitory.

The late edition of Japanese newspaper *Yomiuri Shimbun* reported that, as he was being led away, the luckless burglar declared, 'I'd never have guessed police lived here'.

29 March

2007

'Nassau County Legislator Peter J. Schmitt wants you to be protected from sexual predators', said the headline on the postcard mailed out by Republican politicians in New York state. To that end they included a hotline number which they claimed would warn callers about sexual predators in their neighbourhoods.

'Hey there, sexy guy', said the husky recorded female voice at the end of the hotline. 'Welcome to an exciting new way to go live, one on one, with hot horny girls waiting right now to talk to you.'

'Apparently there was an error in the phone number', admitted Republican spokesman Ed Ward. Instead of 1-800, it should have been 1-888, he admitted. Instead of promoting their 'moral' values, the Republicans had provided free advertising for a phone sex line to thousands of voters. There were no reports of any complaints.

30 March

1975

During a concert for Easter Sunday in Mexico City, Uruguayan conductor José Severier shocked his audience by accidentally stabbing himself through the hand with his baton. Although blood was spraying out of his wound on to his white shirt and shoes, the brave maestro carried on until the end of the performance. It was only later that he revealed that the baton had broken into pieces and that 'one piece was sticking though my hand. Ironically,' he added, 'I never use a baton. But I decided to use one for this performance because I thought it would help me achieve greater musical control. That was a mistake.'

31 March

1990

John Smoltz, one of the most successful pitchers in the recent history of baseball, was still a comparatively new face on the scene in 1990, but he quickly rose to fame thanks to the discovery of five inch-long welts on his body. It wasn't the burn marks so much as his explanation of how they ended up there that drew attention. It was reported that Smoltz said he got them while ironing a shirt – a shirt that he was wearing at the time. 'I've ironed that way five or six times,' he is supposed to have said, 'and never had it happen. I couldn't believe it.'

It's worth noting that Smoltz has since vehemently denied the story, suggesting that it's a particularly ridiculous urban myth – a response that has led more than one wit to suggest that it's almost certainly true.

1912

The annual and hugely competitive Oxford and Cambridge boat race came to an abrupt end when both boats sank. Trouble started for Oxford when their boat started taking on water. The team made for bank and successfully upturned the boat and got back in, only to discover that one of their oarsmen was missing. 'I spotted a chum called Boswell', was the explanation he gave for his prolonged absence. Once they finally got back out into the water, the Oxford crew were alarmed to see the Cambridge eight whizzing past them – not least because they were all swimming: their boat was underwater. When the Oxford boat once again began to take on water, the race was abandoned for the first and only time in its long history.

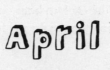

April

1 April

A student at Barry University in Miami informed police that she was woken up by strange noises coming from her closet. Upon further investigation she claimed to have found a University of Miami American football star, Najeh Davenport, 'making dung' in her laundry basket.

Davenport was arrested but was eventually released without charge, thanks to a plea bargain in which he agreed to teach his sport at a number of clinics. His defence lawyer summed up the result beautifully: 'Thanks to the plea deal, it won't be necessary for us to dig to the bottom of this situation, and we're just going leave it where it was.'

2 April

2007

Chameleons are, of course, best known for their ability to change their colour and make themselves hard to see. Dragos Radovic, a 25-year-old from Serbia, knowing that that there was a thriving black market in the rare lizards, thought he might be able to put these camouflaging talents to good use. His plan was simple: the animals would hide themselves as he went through customs.

So he was surprised when he was arrested at Bangkok airport on the way back from Thailand with 175 chameleons in his luggage. Security had been alerted to the fact that something was amiss when they saw his bag moving. When they opened it, they saw the reptiles clear as day. During the long flight they had become dehydrated and distressed and so lost their ability to change colour.

Radovic was most disappointed, and complained to reporters: 'The man who sold them said they changed colour to make themselves invisible against any background, but it didn't work.'

3 April

1988

Veteran parachutist Ivan McGuire made an elementary error when filming his students skydiving: he jumped out of the plane without a parachute on his back. A video camera attached to his helmet recorded his final moments as he made the 2-mile descent and his final words when he realized his mistake. 'Uh-oh', he said.

The official verdict was death by misadventure. 'A man who has jumped 800 times ought to remember his parachute', said police, correctly but not particularly helpfully.

4 April

2003

Firemen spent three long, wet, cold hours attempting to rescue a cow from the River Derwent in the English Peak District. Once the animal was safely on land, they started packing up their equipment and watched in horror as the animal jumped right back into the water.

5 April

1994

A DJ for radio station KYNG-FM in Dallas, Texas, was concerned that his local library in Fort Worth was underused. His worry was that books weren't getting the respect that they deserved and people in the area just weren't reading enough.

To solve the problem, he hit on the idea of luring more people into the library by hiding $100 around the building, inserting notes inside books in the fiction section. He announced that he'd hidden the money on air, just after five o'clock this afternoon, having neglected to forewarn the staff in the library. The first they knew of it was when chaos broke out in their hitherto silent sanctuary.

Library spokeswoman Marsha Anderson said she was getting ready to leave for home when the first people started pouring through the door and shouting, 'Where's fiction? Where's fiction?'

'Books were sailing, and elbows were flying, and people were climbing the shelves', she said. Dr Jack C. Scott, a psychologist from a nearby university counselling centre, declared that 'it was massive hysteria, a massive reaction in which there was a kind of contagion in the air. It was completely unstructured and irrational.'

Soon there were more than 500 people in the building, convinced that as much as $10,000 was at stake. A spokesman for the radio station could only say that he had 'no idea' where the vastly inflated figure had come from.

The peace of the library was completely shattered. 'They started climbing on each other, and books became airborne', said Anderson. The crowd ripped through the books, tearing out pages and breaking spines. In the end more than 3,500 volumes were pulled off the shelves and scattered over the floor.

The librarians at first tried to contact the KYNG-FM radio station and convince them to call off the mob over the airwaves but were unable to reach them. Order was finally restored only when one of the staff hit on the clever idea of announcing (falsely) that the cash had been discovered and the contest was over.

6 April

2007

The plan to bust Timothy Rouse from his high-security prison in Kentucky was absurd. His friend simply walked into a local grocery store and sent a fax to the prison authorities claiming to have come from the state supreme court and 'demanding' that they set Rouse free right away. The fax was apparently riddled with spelling and grammatical errors and had no official letterhead or stamp. In fact, the name of the shop could clearly be seen on the paper.

The craziest thing about the whole scheme, however, was the fact that it worked. Rouse had only just been incarcerated for assault as well as various robbery charges and was considered a dangerous prisoner, but he was set free almost as soon as the dodgy fax was received. The director of the prison later said, most interestingly, that the fax did not arouse any suspicion because bad spelling is so common in official court documents anyway. He did admit, however, that if someone had traced the source of the fax, 'in hindsight, that would perhaps have caused somebody to ask a question'.

It took two weeks for anyone to realize that a mistake had been made, whereupon Rouse was immediately re-arrested. Perhaps not a genius himself, he was found at his mother's house watching TV.

7 April

1998

A 32-year-old German camper died from injuries received when he tried to light a cigarette in a campsite toilet. The toilet exploded and blew him out through a closed window.

1832

Today Joseph Thomson, a farmer from the Lake District, finally grew tired of his wife. He'd been married to her for three years and, as he announced in the market square in Carlisle, 'she has been to me only a born serpent. I took her for my comfort, and the good of my home; but she became my tormentor, a domestic curse, a night invasion, and a daily devil.'

Unfortunately, history doesn't record what Mrs Thomson thought of Joseph, nor her reaction to his rather unusual method of getting rid of her: selling her to the highest bidder. Thomson, obviously something of a salesman, delineated her qualities thus: 'She can make butter and scold the maid; she can sing Moore's melodies, and plait her frills and caps; she cannot make rum, gin, or whisky, but she is a good judge of the quality from long experience in tasting them. I therefore offer her with all her perfections and imperfections, for the sum of 50 shillings.'

In the end, however, he was forced to knock the price down to 20 shillings and a Newfoundland dog, offered by one Henry Mears, who agreed to take Mrs Thomson home. Sadly, history is also silent about how the new couple got along.

8 April

1795

Early in 1795 the future George IV agreed to an arranged marriage with his cousin Caroline of Brunswick, in return for having his debts paid off by his father. Their initial meeting was something of a bust. George's words on seeing his bride-to-be were: 'I am not very well, pray get me a glass of brandy.' This awkward encounter had nothing on the actual wedding day, however. The Prince spent it blind drunk, ignoring his bride and making obscene gestures to his mistress, until he collapsed unconscious into a fireplace, where he spent the night.

After this unpleasant occasion George never managed to over-come his aversion to Caroline's 'personal nastiness', and the two went their separate ways, doing nothing to disguise their mutual loathing. Years later, when Napoleon Bonaparte died, a messenger rushed to the King and told him: 'Your majesty, your greatest enemy is dead.' 'Is she by God?' asked George, before realizing that the eager envoy was referring to the man he'd been at war with for decades, rather than his wife.

9 April

1865

Virginia farmer Wilmer McLean was understandably upset when the American Civil War started in his backyard. The farmer's fields were the site of the First Battle of Bull Run on 18 July 1861 and suffered considerable damage. Meanwhile, artillery fired at McLean's house and a cannonball dropped through his kitchen fireplace.

Shortly after these upsetting events, he moved 120 miles south to Appomattox County, hoping that by doing so he would protect his family from the further ravages of war. He managed to live rel-atively quietly until 9 April 1865, when the conflict came back to him with a bang. The famous Battle of Appomattox was fought just outside his property. When it was all over, his house was requi-sitioned so that Confederate General Robert E. Lee had some-where to sign documents of surrender to Union General Ulysses Grant.

'The war started in my backyard and ended in my parlour', McLean later said ruefully. He was no doubt made all the more bitter by the knowledge that, almost as soon as the historic sur-render document was signed, those present stripped his house bare, taking away just about everything that couldn't be tied down as souvenirs.

10 April

2007

When she went away on holiday, Elaine Bell's last words to her teenage daughter Rachael were 'I don't want any kids or drink in the house'. That Rachael adopted a rather flexible interpretation of this request was evidenced when an advertisement appeared on her Myspace webpage inviting all and sundry to come round for a 'trash the average family-sized house all-night party'.

More than 200 turned up and proceeded to wreck Rachael's mother's clothes, urinate on beds and carpets, spray graffiti on the walls and vomit just about everywhere. The party ended only in the small hours, after enraged neighbours had chased partygoers away from their affluent middle-class enclave with golf clubs and police sealed off the street. The damage was estimated at £20,000.

'I totally regret it', said Rachael.

11 April

1994

Tamara Jo Klemowsky was lucky to be alive after she fell out of the window of a bus travelling at 55 m.p.h. She got away with just a few broken bones and perhaps a regretful sense that the accident need not have happened. Had she not decided to moon the car behind the bus, and had she not pressed her bare buttocks quite so hard against the window, it might not have given way.

12 April

2005

When more than £11,000 of damage was done to a line of brand new 4 x 4 vehicles parked in a Pembrokeshire field, police were quick to blame local vandals. They changed their diagnosis when Claude Brevost, a worker from the garage that owned the cars, went into the same field and was attacked by a ram.

The sheep had entered the paddock that the garage was using as overflow for its fleet of Land Rovers through a broken fence and was now attacking everything that moved, alarmed at the prospect of a love rival during the mating season. 'Everything that moved' included the animal's own reflection, which it could see in the shining paintwork of the new Land Rovers.

So it was that large dents were left in the bodywork of the cars and the amorous ram-raider got a sore head. Meanwhile, according to the owner of the garage, Claude escaped from his encounter without suffering too much damage. 'He ended up a bit bruised . . . but at least it solved the mystery for us.'

13 April

2007

Schoolteacher Maite Larrondo came to regret criticizing the mayor of La Cruz in Chile. First, the vengeful mayor sacked him; then he told him he had been reassigned to a new post. That this new job wasn't necessarily desirable became clear to the teacher when he reported for work in the mayor's office. 'When I asked what my job was going to be, they simply told me to stare at a wall. I then put my desk in front of the wall and have looked at it since then', he said, seven days after he got the new desk job.

Once news leaked out, local officials moved quickly to remove the mayor. Few could disagree with local MP Marco Henríquez Ominami's assessment of the situation. 'This is a weird case', he said.

2005

US President George W. Bush had a message for the American Super Bowl champions, the New England Patriots. 'I want to thank you for the importance that you've shown for education and literacy', he said.

14 April

1999

Alan Rashid was sentenced to two years in prison for making a threat to kill someone after a cough obscured the word 'not' when the jury foreman read out a verdict of 'not guilty'. 'You have not pleaded guilty to this crime and you showed no remorse', said the judge when carrying out the sentencing, and Mr Rashid was led out in handcuffs.

It was only when a member of the jury politely asked a court usher what a man they'd declared innocent was doing waiting for a van to take him to prison that it was realized just how ill-timed the cough had been.

'Mr Rashid was a very relieved man when the judge explained what had happened', said a court spokesman. 'It was all very bizarre.'

1912

The 'unsinkable' ship the HMS *Titanic* sank.

15 April

1984

Fez-wearing pratfalling comedian Tommy Cooper died on air in front of millions of TV viewers while taking part in the ITV variety show *Live from Her Majesty's*. Most of the audience thought his collapse was a joke and carried on laughing until the orchestra started playing and his prone form was dragged backstage.

While clearly a sad event, this was a fitting end to a career that began in remarkably similar circumstances. Cooper had made his stage début at the age of seventeen at a public concert in the canteen of his shipping firm in Essex. His plan had been to give a serious magic show, but when he walked into the lights he forgot all his lines and proceeded to perform every trick incorrectly. His finale was the famous milk bottle trick. The basic scheme of this conjuror's favourite is that you take a full open bottle of milk, place paper over the top, turn it upside down, remove the paper and the milk magically stays in. But when Cooper took away the paper, all the milk came out and he was drenched – much to the delight of the audience. Even more pleasing to them was his subsequent display of stage fright, which left him standing wordless on the stage, furiously moving his mouth but with no sound coming out. It was only when he walked off to the wings and heard the cheering that he realized he might have a future in show business after all . . .

1998

Two elderly Germans took a wrong turn while driving their electric wheelchairs outside their retirement home in Bonn and ended up on the motorway. Police rescued the confused pensioners after motorists complained about the slow-moving wheelchairs holding up rush-hour traffic.

16 April

2003

When reviewing the strange events of this morning in 2003, 71-year-old Andreas Janik said, 'I thought a bomb had dropped. There was a loud crash and then I felt something hit the bed.'

That something turned out to be a two-ton wild boar, which had been chased into the German man's home by a Yorkshire terrier. Terrified of the diminutive dog, it had crashed through Mr Janik's patio doors and was now attempting to hide itself under his sheets, much to Mr Janik's alarm.

'I sat up, and there was a wild pig in the bed, tusks and everything, trying to hide under the duvet', he said. 'My wife and I leaped out of the bed, and we saw the dog outside barking, and we had to chase it off before we could persuade the pig to leave.'

He continued: 'I had to hit it on the snout with a newspaper. I can't believe it was afraid of such a little dog.'

1912

The UK's paper of record, *The Times*, led with the headline '*Titanic* Sunk', followed by the reassuring but decidedly inaccurate words 'No Lives Lost'.

17 April

2000

Christine Allery, the woman who had moved into the house of the recently deceased William Reynolds, was surprised to receive a letter sent to him by Lambeth City Council.

'Your council tax benefit has been stopped from 17 April 2000 because there has been a change in your circumstances', the letter informed Mr Reynolds, a victim of cancer. 'The change is because you are dead.'

Mr Reynolds was at least given a chance to protest against this decision. 'If you think you still qualify for benefit, you must contact this office immediately to obtain a new application form', the letter continued.

18 April

2007

It isn't exactly clear what Johann Stark was after when he broke into a sports club in Aachen, but the mistake he made was as clear as day to everyone for miles around. A police spokesman explained: 'He had no torch and turned on the first light switch that he could find – the switch to the floodlights of the club's football pitch.'

Spotting this sudden illumination from his nearby house, the club's groundsman immediately called the police, and they hurried round to arrest the light-fingered thief.

19 April

1912

Gertrude Stein is now remembered as one of the most important figures in the Modernist movement in literature, famous for her association with Ernest Hemingway, F. Scott Fitzgerald, James Joyce, Ezra Pound and T. S. Eliot, as well as for her own pioneering writing. It was she who invented the sobriquet 'The Lost Generation' for the young men returning from the First World War, and it was she who famously once declared, 'Rose is a rose is a rose is a rose'.

However, fame was a long time coming for Stein, and throughout her life she had many detractors, thanks to her repetitive and often impenetrable prose style, full of repetitions, back-trackings, hugely long sentences, repetitions that irritate, sentences that are too long, long in length . . . you get the idea.

The most cutting criticism of all, however, came early on in her career from an editor she had rather hoped would publish her work. Dated 19 April 1912, his letter of rejection ran as follows:

Dear Madam,

I am only one, only one, only one. Only one being, one at the same time. Not two, not three, only one. Only one life to live, only sixty minutes in one hour. Only one pair of eyes. Only one brain. Only one being. Being only one, having only one pair of eyes, having only one life, I cannot read your MS three or four times. Not even one time. Only one look, only one look is enough. Hardly one copy would sell here. Hardly one. Hardly one. Many thanks. I am returning the MS by registered post. Only one MS by one post.

Sincerely yours,
A. C. Field

1902

The UK League Cup football final ended in a score-draw. The Sheffield Utd goalkeeper, William 'Fatty' Foulke, was unhappy with the result. Unable to contain his annoyance after the game, the huge player (who was thought to have weighed more than 20 stone and is reputed to have been the original inspiration for the famous soccer chant 'Who ate all the pies?'), emerged stark naked from the dressing-room and angrily pursued the match referee, who took refuge in a broom cupboard and had to be rescued by other officials.

20 April

2004

Like their counterparts all over the world, Canadian Highway Patrolmen are well used to arresting drivers who are swerving all over the road. What was unusual on this occasion, however, was that the car's erratic progress had been caused by the fact that its owner had been playing the violin when driving. His protests that he was only practising for an important concert fell on tone-deaf ears and he was led away. The arresting officer commented later that it was 'lucky he didn't play the cello'.

21 April

1955

When a gold nugget was found in Minas Gerais State in Argentina, prospectors rushed to the spot. As fast as they could, they dug and dug and soon had created a huge trench. Unfortunately, they discovered nothing apart from the fact that it's a good idea to shore up the foundations of any mine workings properly. Soon after they had tunnelled forty foot down, with no more gold having been found, their excavations collapsed and thirty men were buried alive.

22 April

1778

Whitehaven is now a pretty small town on the west coast of Cumbria, but once it was one of England's most important ports – which is why, back in 1778, it became the last place on the English mainland to be raided successfully from the sea.

The event took place during the American War of Independence, when John Paul Jones, a locally trained adventurer who had fled to the US colonies after being accused of brutality and murder aboard a ship in the West Indies, returned to his old home to exact revenge.

Jones used his knowledge of local habits to catch the lazy town garrison napping, literally. He split his men into two groups, and they stole into the harbour by moonlight. The group that he was with took the sleeping guards prisoner, destroyed the harbour guns and successfully burned a ship.

'On my return from this business I naturally expected to see the fire of the ships on the north side as well as to find my own party with everything in readiness to set fire to the shipping in the south', he wrote in his log-book. However, his plans had gone awry. He had forgotten one of the town's other great characteristics: a wild passion for drink.

While he had been working over the garrison, the other half of his landing party had been tempted into the Red Lion tavern by the harbour side and spent the night downing huge quantities of the local grog. They stayed so long that all their torches burned down, meaning that, even if they'd wanted to, they wouldn't have been able to start any fires. Jones recorded ruefully in his log that the men eventually returned to him in a state of 'some confusion'.

Once he'd loaded his drink-sodden crew on board, they beat an ignominious retreat as the sun rose and the outraged citizens of the port, finally waking, poured down to the harbour after them.

John Paul Jones went on to become the founding father of the US Navy and one of the New World's first celebrity heroes.

23 April

1998

Lanny Frattare, a baseball broadcaster, broke into game coverage to deliver a moving eulogy to James Earl Jones. He informed his listeners that the veteran actor had just passed away and waxed nostalgic about his leading role in the classic baseball film *Field of Dreams*. 'A lot of us in baseball have a lot of feelings about *Field of Dreams* and the soliloquy he gave in it', Frattare said.

Minutes later, Frattare had to interrupt coverage of the game again to inform the fans that James Earl Jones was, in fact, still alive. He'd misheard an announcement from his producer, who had in fact told him that James Earl Ray, the assassin of Martin Luther King, had just cashed his final cheque.

'I don't feel glad about it; in fact I feel like a real fool', Frattare said.

24 April

1991

Today Gerald Ratner, the tycoon head of Britain's biggest jewellery business, woke up to discover that the good-humoured speech he'd made the night before had landed him in a spot of bother. Ratner had been speaking after lunch to Britain's venerable Institute of Directors and needed to keep the delegates awake. So he'd decided to crack a few jokes.

He started off by explaining that, yes, it was remarkable that his firm could sell ear-rings for 99p – less than the price of a Marks and Spencer prawn sandwich – but not all that impressive really if you considered that they probably wouldn't last as long as the M&S product.

'We also do cut-glass sherry decanters,' he added, 'complete with six glasses on a silver-plated tray that your butler can serve you drinks on, all for £4.95. People say, "How can you sell this for such a low price?" I say, because it's total crap.'

The comments may have seemed funny to Ratner at the time, but the laughter no doubt stuck in his throat when they hit the headlines all over the UK the following morning. Within a year his company's profits of £111 million had turned into a loss of £122 million, and Ratner had been forced to leave the board of his own company.

'Up to that point everything had been going swimmingly', Ratner told *The Guardian* years later. 'In fact an analyst had asked me the day before what could possibly go wrong. I said I had no idea and yet a day later it had all gone wrong. I don't blame anyone for what went wrong other than myself', he added nobly. 'I certainly don't blame the press. I handed the story to them on a silver platter, if you'll excuse the pun.'

25 April

1989

Italian MP and former pornographic actress La Cicciolina returned to Kiskunhalas, her native village in Hungary, to celebrate the withdrawal of the Soviet troops that had occupied the land there since 1945. As a symbolic gesture, she released a white dove in front of the assembled media representatives, who all watched in horror as the bird flew on to a wholly unsuitable perch on a railway transporter's loading ramp and was run over by a tank.

26 April

2007

Distinguished alumni gathered for the opening of a fifty-year-old time capsule at the University of Washington were surprised when the first thing they saw when the lid was lifted was a centrefold spread from a pornographic magazine. The box was also found to contain copies of *Playboy* and *Hustler* magazines, an antique condom, items of underwear (which had clearly been used), several dried up chocolate bars and an April Fool's edition of a student magazine from the 1970s.

As one of the older attendees correctly pointed out, these artefacts were not part of the original collection (which also, fortunately, survived). 'I just think this is a great college prank', department chair Gerald Baldasty said, putting a brave face on things. 'We're not upset at all; we're just having a good chuckle over it.'

27 April

2006

Today, the notoriously hard-living guitarist Keith Richards proved that he wasn't afraid to get out of his tree, even at the venerable age of sixty-two. But this time the tree in question wasn't metaphorical. It was a real coconut palm on the luxury resort of Wakaya in Fiji.

Richards was said to have been ferreting around for coconuts with his fellow Rolling Stones member Charlie Watts, when he took a tumble and landed on his head. Reports at the time claimed that the famously unflappable rocker complained of a slight headache, but nothing bad enough to prevent him from taking a quick spin on a jet-ski – and getting into another accident.

It was only after this second fall that Richards – who was then just three years under the age requirement for getting a free bus pass – agreed to see a doctor. He subsequently had to undergo an operation to have a blood clot removed from his brain but fortunately suffered no long-lasting ill effects – other than the hole in his wallet caused by the fact that the accident forced the Rolling Stones to postpone a multi-million pound tour.

28 April

1992

The 69-year-old Jose Rodriguez was charged with reckless driving and driving without a licence after he put nine pedestrians into hospital. Witnesses described how he backed on to a pavement in the middle of Manhattan – at speed – and flung two pedestrians into a glass door. He then lurched into forward gear and hit the road at around 40 m.p.h. before making an abrupt right turn – straight into the window of a record store, via another seven pedestrians.

According to his nephew, the elderly Mr Rodriguez had not wanted to take command of the car – not least because he didn't know how to drive. The vehicle had been parked at a kerb, with Mr Rodriguez sitting in the passenger seat waiting for the driver to return. He'd only – reluctantly – taken the wheel after being repeatedly ordered to do so by a traffic cop who was unhappy with the way that the car was parked.

29 April

1998

A Kenyan couple got into difficulties during an illicit liaison. A freak seizure on the woman's part caused them to become stuck together during the course of their lovemaking, much like mating dogs. This event, and a subsequent call for an ambulance, only signalled the start of their misery.

The two – apparently a local policeman and the wife of a tribal elder – were taken to a local hospital. According to the *Kenyan Times*, when news of their situation spread, 'thousands of excited residents thronged the hospital'. So many indeed, that they 'paralysed all activity in the town'.

The couple cannot have been made more comfortable by the knowledge that their adultery had been discovered, nor that 'scores of dwellers, young and old', were thronging to the hospital to catch a glimpse of their strange encounter. They must have felt even worse when they heard police firing tear gas to disperse the crowd.

The newspaper said that they were finally flown to Nairobi to be separated. Sadly, it did not report on whether their respective marriages had survived such a sticky situation.

30 April

2000

Deputy Sheriff Gamaliel 'Tony' Dominguez became violently ill soon after eating a Burger King 'whopper' on 30 April 2002. He had asked for a burger without any sauce or pickle – a request that had so annoyed chef Daniel Musson that he'd laced the burger with a special sauce of his own devising: oven cleaner.

At his subsequent trial Musson explained: 'I thought it'd be funny, and it was a cool thing to do at the time.' The judge disagreed, and he was sent to jail.

May

1 May

2004

Gary Johnson, the boss of Yeovil Town football club, named his team's May Day game against Hull City as the biggest in the history of the club. If they won it, they'd qualify for the all-important play-offs and stand a chance of promotion into the big league of English soccer. In spite of these considerations, Mike Bromfield's reaction to hearing about the game could be considered excessive. Especially since he was told on a satellite phone when 17,000 feet up Mount Everest. The 55-year-old tour guide immediately stopped his ascent of the mountain, hiked for three days through raging blizzards, got into a tiny plane that took him to Kathmandu, got another flight from there to Heathrow and rushed down to Somerset from London. He arrived just in time to watch his team lose 2–1.

2 May

2004

'Splash Day' is one of the highlights of the year at the Hippie Hollow nudist beach in Texas. It's the time that thousands of gays and lesbians from the otherwise intolerant state of Texas tear off their clothes and go for a well-deserved cool-off in the waters of Lake Travis.

Rather a bigger splash than had been anticipated was made in 2004, however. A double-decker barge carrying tourists along the lake hit trouble when all sixty passengers rushed over to the Hippie Hollow side of the boat hoping to see some nudie lesbian action. The weight of all those tourists gawping at naked bodies knocked the boat off balance and ejected them into 'about 39 feet of water' as the Travis County sheriff, Roger Wade, later explained.

Fortunately, no one was seriously hurt, not least because naked party-goers from the resort rushed in and rescued the struggling voyeurs.

1964

'Am I dying, or is it my birthday?' asked Lady Nancy Astor when she woke to see a crowd of relatives around her bed. She was dying – and those were her last words.

3 May

1993

An initiation rite for 'Mountain Men Anonymous', a rafting club based in Oregon, went awry when, instead of shooting a beer can off his friend Tony Roberts's head with a hunting arrow, Michael Kennedy shot him in the eye.

Doctors gave a graphic description of how the arrow went through Roberts's right eye and burrowed eight inches into his brain. They also said that if the arrow had gone one millimetre to the left, Roberts would definitely have died. He would also have died if he'd tried to pull the arrow out himself, instead of waiting patiently for the ambulance with it still lodged in his cranium.

'I feel so dumb about this', said Roberts, who suffered no (further) loss of brain function.

4 May

1990

A nudist camp near Trieste proved to be the literal downfall of three hang-glider enthusiasts. When they spotted a number of attractive young women on the ground beneath them, the three started circling around the camp, eyes firmly fixed on the nubile creatures – so firmly that they forgot to take account of each other. They collided in mid-air, falling on the sand in front of the surprised bathing beauties, sustaining a variety of unpleasant injuries and considerably wounded pride.

5 May

1999

It's widely acknowledged that being a petrol station attendant isn't the most interesting job in the world, especially in those dull pre-dawn hours. So few would blame the man who fell asleep on the job in Tortosa in Spain on this quiet morning in 1999.

Indeed, local drivers certainly didn't complain when they saw that he had nodded off. They called their friends instead and told them to come and fill up their cars. More than £500 worth of petrol had been quietly siphoned off before police realized what was going on, alerted by the long line of cars, which, as an officer told Reuters, 'was very odd at that time'.

Naturally, the attendant was very upset when he realized what had happened, but the real kick in the teeth came when the police who had come to wake him realized that they wanted him for another crime and arrested him.

6 May

1902

After burning ashes gushed out by Mount Pelee fell on the town of St Pierre in Martinique, the Mayor had some advice for his citizens: 'Do not allow yourself to fall victim to groundless panic', he said in reassuring tones. 'Please allow us to advise you to return to your normal occupations.' He was backed up by his local governor, who was anxious to keep the voters in the town for an important upcoming election. The conclusion of a recent commission of inquiry into the volcano also declared, 'The safety of St Pierre is absolutely assured.'

On 8 May the volcano erupted, wiping out the town and killing all but two of its 30,000 inhabitants.

7 May

2001

Not unreasonably, Arnold Ancheta didn't like it in jail. His time in the medium-security Elmwood Correctional Facility, near San Jose, was no fun at all. He wanted out.

His attempt to escape can't be faulted for determination. As officials later explained, he stood on his bunk bed and punched holes in the walls of his cell to use as steps to climb up to a skylight. When he finally reached this small outlet, he used a bed sheet and mop handle to prize apart the bars that covered it. He then squeezed through the metal bars and, demonstrating considerable dexterity and strength, balanced on them while he broke the Perspex covering on the roof window.

Once he was on the outside, he made a daring 20-foot leap to the ground and started running. Unfortunately, however, instead of heading for a fence that led to the road and freedom, he took a wrong turn and climbed a different barrier – one that took him out of the frying pan and into the fire. He touched down in the female side of his jail. There he ran around the yard for a while in a state of considerable confusion until he was spotted by inmates, reported to the authorities and immediately taken away to a higher-security institution.

8 May

1936

Spectators at Bay Meadows racecourse, near San Francisco in California, were horrified to watch as popular nineteen-year-old jockey Ralph Neves crashed through a fence, fell from his horse and was trampled under the feet of four others. Shortly afterwards, silence fell as the race announcer informed the crowd that he was dead.

Doctors in the hospital had been unable to do anything for Neves, and he was toe-tagged and sent down to the morgue. And that's where he awoke several minutes later, bloodied, shirtless, covered from head to toe in a morgue sheet and wearing just one shoe. In a state of understandable confusion he hailed a cab and hurried back to the racetrack.

The crowd greeted his arrival at the course with considerable excitement, doing their best to grab him as he sprinted under the bandstand, still wearing his toe-tag, still dripping blood and still half naked. 'At one point', he said later, 'I think everyone on the damn track was chasing me.'

He shook off his pursuers, however, and burst into the jockeys' room, where his friends were in the process of holding a collection for his bereaved widow – who fainted when she saw him back from the dead, standing in the doorway and demanding to be allowed to ride. In spite of his insistence that he didn't feel dead, race organizers refused to let him get back in the saddle again. On 9 May, however, he was pronounced well enough to compete and went on to ride five winners.

9 May

1864

John B. Sedgwick, a Confederate General in the US Civil War, considerably underestimated the shooting abilities of his enemy as he looked out over a parapet at enemy lines, prompting the famous last words 'Why, they couldn't hit an elephant at this dist . . .'

10 May

2006

James Ashton of Bury St Edmunds may go down in history as one of the most comically inept bank robbers of all time. His bid for immortality came in his local branch of the Woolwich Building Society. He'd already been into the branch that morning to remove some money from his own account by legitimate means but clearly decided that he hadn't taken enough out because he returned a few hours later.

His only attempt at disguise had been to pull up the hood of his coat, but he had at least rehearsed a fine speech. He told a bemused cashier, 'This is a robbery. I'm drunk. I've got a knife. I want money.'

He then took less money than he had in his account anyway and stumbled out of the branch. Three members of staff were able to identify Mr Ashton to the police – because they were all on first name terms with him – and he was arrested within minutes of leaving the building.

11 May

2006

Supermodel Tatyana Simanava tumbled from a coach travelling at 50 m.p.h. on to a busy New York road when she mistook an exit door for the entrance to the toilet. 'I asked where the bathroom was and I was told it's down the stairs, there's a door', said Ms

Simanava, who is blonde. 'I opened the first door I saw, and I don't remember anything after that.'

It appears that the model was pitched out on to the road immediately upon opening the door. Fortunately no cars hit her, and the driver of the coach, who saw her falling, was able to pull over immediately. She suffered nothing worse than bruising to her arm and jaw and becoming the subject of endless bad jokes about the colour of her hair.

1812

Spencer Perceval became the first British Prime Minister to be assassinated when he was shot in the Houses of Parliament. Interestingly, just after the bullet hit him, he said: 'I'll have one of Bellamy's veal pies!' Then he fell to the ground, dead.

12 May

2002

Police were called out to calm down a noisy altercation in the street next to a pick-up truck in Edmonton, Canada. When they arrived, they saw a man and woman fleeing down the street, the woman pulling up her trousers and the man bleeding from his hand. Inside the truck, the officers found blood, clumps, blonde hair and a finger. When they caught up with her, the woman explained to police that she was a prostitute and had bitten the finger off the man when he refused to pay her. The man himself managed to run away, but police were easily able to track him down because his name and company's phone number were written on the door of his truck.

'There's a lot of lessons here and they're all really apparent', said Wes Bellmore, spokesman for the Edmonton police.

13 May

1983

On this Friday the 13th in 1983, two peat cutters dug up a body in a Wilmslow bog. Peter Reyn-Bardt, whom police had suspected of killing his wife since she had disappeared without a trace in the 1950s, almost immediately confessed to putting it there.

The body was then sent to Oxford University, where it was discovered to date from around AD 250. Nevertheless Reyn-Bardt was convicted of murder and sent to jail. Meanwhile, police continued hunting for the body and soon discovered another corpse. This one dated from 300 BC. Mrs Reyn-Bardt was never found.

14 May

964

Popes, like all members of the Roman Catholic clergy, take a solemn vow of chastity. They are also, according to long-held doctrine, infallible and the representative of God on earth. And that's why the death of Pope John XII causes such problems for the faithful. He expired in the bed of one of his many mistresses, bludgeoned to death after her jealous husband had caught His Holiness ministering 'sexual affections' on her. Ever since, the priapic pontiff has been known as John the Bad.

15 May

1918

The world's first air-mail flight on 15 May 1918 was a grand event. President Woodrow Wilson himself was among the notables who waited in Washington's Potomac Park to watch the plane take off. And they had a long wait.

The first problem was the late arrival of the pilot, George Boyle, a man who unkind critics said only got such a prestigious job because he was engaged to the daughter of an Interstate Commerce commissioner, and who, they also said, was a complete doofus. When Boyle finally arrived and the 150-pound mailbag had been loaded alongside him into the cockpit of his single-engine Curtis Jenny, another problem arose. The plane wouldn't start. Mechanics spent over half an hour tinkering with the engine and propeller before someone thought to look in the fuel tank – and discovered it was empty.

Finally, once enough fuel had been siphoned off from other planes on the field, Boyle tried the switch to engine on again. This time the propeller turned, and the plane took off – in completely the wrong direction. Instead of flying north to his intended destination in Pennsylvania, Boyle careered away due south. He realized his error 25 miles out of Washington and attempted to land in a cornfield so he could ask directions . . . Unfortunately he landed the wrong way round, flipped the plane over as he taxied along the impromptu runway and damaged it beyond repair.

The mail was removed from the wrecked aircraft and delivered to Philadelphia by road.

1954

Eddie Bond turned down Elvis Presley in an audition. 'Stick with driving a truck,' he told the youngster, 'you're never going to make it as a singer'. A few months later Elvis had his first hit with 'That's Alright Mama'. Bond asked him if he wanted to join his band. Elvis politely declined. His singing career went on to be notably successful (Presley's, that is).

16 May

1999

When the Bambrick family from the West Midlands heard high-pitched screams, frantic scratching and tortured moans emerging from the very walls of their house, they feared the worst. When they next discovered what appeared to be a black cross on their hearth rug, their suspicions were confirmed. They were being haunted by a poltergeist.

Immediately, they took the only reasonable course that they could think of and got the local priest in. Sadly, however, his holy blessings failed to dislodge the spectral visitor, and the Bambricks were forced to abandon their home.

It was only when paterfamilias John Bambrick returned on 17 May that he realized that they may have acted hastily. A pile of soot that had fallen on the floor next to his gas fire prompted him to call in the gas man – who discovered a large ginger cat stuck on a ledge half-way up the chimney.

Mr Bambrick was relieved to inform the local press that the cat was alive and well in spite of its five-day ordeal, and added ruefully, 'We were convinced the house was haunted by a poltergeist but feel a bit daft now'.

17 May

1980

'No one knows more about this mountain than Harry, and it don't dare blow up on him.' Sadly, Harry Truman's assertion to TV reporters investigating disaster predictions at Mount St Helens in Oregon was proved wrong when the volcano erupted. The explosion was said to be 500 times more powerful than the atomic bomb at Hiroshima. Harry died, along with fifty-nine other people and his seventeen cats.

18 May

1982

It's often said that lawyers will employ any trick at all, and stoop to any level, in order to win a case, but when Florida attorney Steve Jerome tried to win over a jury by singing them an aria, it was generally considered that he'd gone too far.

Jerome was representing one Robert Infante, who was on trial for kicking a dent in a neighbour's car, and sang his closing argument. 'Innocent, or is this man guiiiiilty? He is not guiiiiilty', he wailed to the tune of 'Vesti la giubba' from the opera *I Pagliacci*, his face turning red as he strained for the high notes.

At first the jurors are said to have looked confused. Then a few of them started giggling. Then they all found Infante guilty anyway and fined him $250.

19 May

1725

Johann Beringer, the dean of medicine at the University of Wurzburg, had a very high opinion of his own abilities – so high that he was internationally renowned as much for his arrogance as he was for his skill as an early pioneer in the investigation of fossils.

The train of events that sealed Beringer's reputation for good was set in motion on this day early in the summer of 1725. Back then, scientists were still struggling to work out where fossils came from and would have been astounded to learn that most were actually formed on the bottom of the sea, especially as so many of them were to be found on the top of mountains. Which all goes to explain why, when the religious Beringer found some quite remarkable specimens on his regular trawl for rocks on Mount Eibelstadt near his home in Wurzburg, he leaped to the most obvious conclusion: the shapes in the stones were the work of God Himself.

The rocks he found featured the shapes of plants, animals, shooting stars and, most incredibly of all, Hebrew letters carved in sharp relief. Clearly this was not the work of nature, decided Beringer. Soon he was trumpeting his discovery to the world, feverishly gathering more and more of the incredible stones that kept appearing in the same place on the mountain and preparing an exhaustive, lavishly illustrated book of his discoveries.

Even before the book went to press, critics had pointed out that some of the stones Beringer found showed evidence of chisel marks, but the fact that they were clearly sculptures was not a problem for the great scientist.

'The figures . . . are so exactly fitted to the dimensions of the stones, that one would swear that they are the work of a very meticulous sculptor', he wrote. 'They seem to bear unmistakable indications of the sculptor's knife.' The sculptor was, of course, God, and the discoveries were destined to make Beringer the most famous person on the planet.

Things didn't turn out quite as Beringer was happily predicting, however. Shortly before the book was finished, J. Ignatz Roderick and Georg von Eckhart, colleagues of Beringer's at Wurzburg, came forward claiming that they had actually planted the rocks. Astonishingly they'd gone to all the trouble of making them in order to teach Beringer a lesson about arrogance. They even produced a few rocks of their own to show how easily they could be made.

Beringer was furious. He knew just why these men were attacking him. They were jealous! He dedicated a new section in his book to his colleagues' attempts to 'bring down to the dust all my sacrifices and labours, my very reputation'. Furthermore, he took the men to court to save his 'honour'.

During the course of the case Beringer slowly began to realize that he had been duped. Legend has it that in a fury he dedicated the rest of his fortune to buying up all copies of his beautiful but utterly discredited book so that no one would be able to read it and mock him further. His efforts were in vain, however, because it was republished soon after his death, just so that people could laugh at it anew.

20 May

1974

Cardinal Jean Danielou was a world-respected Catholic theologian, one of the most important leaders of the Church in France and the author of no fewer than fourteen stern books on religious morality. So the French nation was exceedingly surprised on 21 May 1975, when it woke to the news that this paragon of Christian virtue had died the night before of a heart attack – which had struck him down on the stairs of a Paris brothel. The Church explained his presence in a house of ill repute on the grounds that the Cardinal often visited sick people and prostitutes. Meanwhile, the French police explained that he had intended merely to comfort – in an official capacity – a 24-year-old blonde with whom he had an assignation. Godless cynics insisted on drawing their own conclusions, however.

21 May

1993

A Saturday night ruckus outside a pub in Southampton ended particularly badly for one man, who lost his ear. When they arrived to clear up the disturbance, police found the severed organ lying on the pavement. The busy policemen took it back to their station, where they put it in a fridge, packed in ice. They hoped that the owner would turn up to reclaim his missing ear and surgeons could reattach it. The man did indeed turn up, but had to be told that his ear had 'gone off'. The explanation was simple, according to

Detective Inspector Ray Burt: 'It was next to an egg roll and that had gone off as well, so there was nothing we could do.'

22 May

1921

The Steinach operation was a curious surgical procedure, briefly popular towards the beginning of the twentieth century. It was a version of vasectomy pioneered in Vienna, believed to cure impotence and rejuvenate ageing men. The poet W. B. Yeats was one famous beneficiary: his post-operation exploits with the young actress Margot Ruddock earned him the mocking soubriquet 'the gland old man of Irish poetry'.

Another man who swore by the procedure was Albert Wilson, who was so impressed by the operation that he underwent in his seventies that he even agreed to give a lecture at the Albert Hall entitled 'How I Was Made Twenty Years Younger'. Unfortunately, this improving talk was never given. Wilson was found dead in his bed the morning before he was due to perform.

23 May

1997

A Sydney grandfather, Paul Miller, was disturbed to read a notice lamenting his death in his local *Newcastle Herald* newspaper. He was even more upset when he realized that the announcement had been placed by his own son Jason.

The text (which explained that Paul would be a 'much missed, father, grandfather and friend') had been placed by the younger Miller (at a cost of A$16.80) in the hope that he'd be offered bereavement leave from work so that he could get time off to look for another job. Jason's plan went awry, however, when Paul bumped into an old friend in the street – who expressed surprise to see him there and explained about the bad news he'd just read in the paper.

Paul quickly announced to the world that news of his death was premature, saying, 'I am alive and well, but this thing has left me shaken.'

1660

Charles II returned to England to take back the throne. One of the unforeseen consequences of the restoration of monarchy was that Sir Thomas Urquhart was so delighted by the news that he entered into an uncontrollable fit of laughter – and died. In contrast, the scholar John Bigg was so depressed by Charles's return that he renounced the world and went to live in a cave in Buckinghamshire, where he remained for the next thirty years.

24 May

1989

Sonia Sutcliffe, wife of Peter Sutcliffe, the Yorkshire Ripper, was awarded £600,000 in a libel case against the satirical magazine *Private Eye,* which had suggested she had profited from her infamy by selling her story to UK paper the *Daily Mail*. The amount she was granted was a hundred times greater than that awarded to three of Sutcliffe's victims, which prompted the magazine's editor, Ian Hislop, to declare famously, 'If that's justice, I'm a banana'.

1626

In one of the most iniquitous property deals in history Dutchman Peter Minuit exchanged a few pots, pans, fish hooks and scraps of cloth with members of the indigenous population for an island off the coast of North America. Its name? Manhattan.

25 May

2004

A meet-and-greet in Washington D.C. produced the following gem from George W. Bush: 'I'm honoured to shake the hand of a brave Iraqi citizen who had his hand cut off by Saddam Hussein.'

2000

One hundred and sixteen heavily armed troops from Italy's élite Alpini corps landed in Kristianstad in Sweden today, ready to take part in a NATO exercise – much to the puzzlement of local immigration officials, who had no idea that such an exercise was taking place.

The confusion was eventually cleared up when the troops explained their purpose and someone realized that they must have intended to land at Kristiansand in Norway. The troops marched back on to their transport plane and took off again. 'This happens now and then', said airport director Lennart Nilsson. 'There are just a couple of letters – but 250 miles – separating the two cities.'

The Italian paper *Corriere della Sera* was less forgiving, however. It pointed out (not unreasonably) that someone should at least have realized that Sweden is not part of NATO and that even if 'Kristiansand and Kristianstad may sound remarkably similar, . . . that is no excuse for Italy invading Sweden in error'.

It was a mistake so strange that it just had to happen twice . . .

26 May

2002

A fifteen-year-old boy in Michigan invited a few friends around to play pool while his parents were away, a decision that he came to regret when more than sixty of his friends eventually turned up – and accidentally started a fire that burned his family home down.

'We suspect it was just a wild, alcohol-fuelled free-for-all', said Police Chief William Dwyer, making it sound more fun than it probably was.

27 May

2006

An unidentified man walked into Kiev Zoo, declared to the crows standing around the lions that 'God will save me, if he exists' and then lowered himself by a rope into the enclosure. Immediately, a lioness leaped on him and cuffed him to the ground, severing a carotid artery in the process. He died within seconds.

1610

Francois Ravaillac, the killer of French king Henry IV, was put to death. Even though assassinating a monarch is generally guaranteed to annoy some people, historians have long considered the punishment he received excessive. First of all, Ravaillac's right hand, which had held the regicidal knife, was burned in a sulphur fire. Then sections of his skin were ripped apart with red-hot pincers and the wounds were filled with molten lead and boiling oil and resin. His torturers ensured that he still lived all the while, even when they next pulled out his entrails. He finally died when he was pulled apart by four horses. After that, just for good measure, his killers burned him and scattered his ashes to the winds. More than 150 years passed before anyone killed a French king again.

28 May

1986

The town of Hamilton, Ohio, voted to change its name by adding an explanation mark to it. 'Hamilton! . . . It's an attention getter!' explained the Chamber of Commerce president at the time. 'We've found it to be a catchy symbol, something we can build on as part of our overall public relations campaign!' Crazily, however, this fun idea was dismissed by the United States Board on Geographic Names. After an expensive PR and sign-changing campaign Hamilton! was forced to change its name back to plain old Hamilton. Town officials were sanguine about the failure, however, concluding that the acres of free publicity the change generated at least helped them to get across their point about the town!

29 May

2001

Preston Lane and his wife, Veronica, today paid visits to their respective parents. Mrs Lane dropped Preston off at his mother Nita Lane's house and then drove their truck around to her own parents a few miles away.

While she was inside, this truck was spotted by one Harley Hughes, who promptly jumped in and drove off with it. The progress of his opportunistic thieving was impeded, however, by a lack of petrol in the vehicle. Just as he noticed that the fuel gauge was running perilously low, he spotted a man standing in a garden and shouted out to him: 'My truck's almost out of gas. Can I borrow some?'

The man wasn't keen on lending, however. As he explained later, the primary thought running through his head was 'Hey! That's my truck!' By bizarre coincidence Hughes had pulled up at Nita Lane's house and started talking to none other than her son Preston.

Preston discreetly arranged for his mother to call the local sheriff while he detained Hughes in the driveway.

Hughes was understandably surprised when the man in blue arrived from out of the blue, and even more perplexed when he was told that the truck he was sitting in belonged to the man from whom he had just tried to borrow petrol. Hughes insisted it couldn't, explaining that he'd taken the truck from a house miles away, which he knew belonged to Jerry Mullins . . . Just at that moment Mullins pulled up with Veronica in the passenger seat. 'That's his father-in-law', the sheriff explained. 'You're shitting me', was Hughes's eloquent response.

30 May

1942

John Barrymore (grandfather of the currently famous Drew) was reckoned to be one of the finest Hamlets of his generation and one of the biggest box-office draws from the early years of Hollywood. He also had a notorious reputation as a hard-drinking ladies' man. Typical of his swashbuckling career was the occasion he wandered, drunk, into a ladies' toilet. Nonplussed by the lack of urinal, he hit on the clever solution of emptying his bladder on a potted plant. An alarmed female patron reminded him that the room was 'for ladies exclusively', whereupon the star of a classic early version of *Moby Dick* and swashbuckling epic *Don Juan* turned around, tackle still in hand, and replied, 'So, madam, is this. But every now and again, I'm compelled to run a little water through it.'

It was on his death in May 1942, however, that Barrymore really entered the realm of legend. The build-up was impressive enough. When a priest came to administer last rites and asked for a final confession, the actor informed him that he was at that moment having 'lustful carnal thoughts'. When the priest asked him about whom, he screamed 'about HER', gesturing to his horrified nurse.

He topped this off with the memorable last words: 'Die? I should say not, dear fellow. No Barrymore would allow such a conventional thing to happen to him.'

But it was the after-events that proved the old rake had lost none of his power to shock. When they heard the sad news of their friend's passing, his fellow hell-raising matinee idol Errol Flynn and renowned actor Raoul Walsh gathered in a bar with a few buddies to commiserate. Walsh soon made his excuses, claiming he was too upset to carry on drinking. Instead of going home, however, he went to the funeral parlour, where he bribed the attendants to let him take Barrymore's body. He then took it round to Errol Flynn's mansion, propped it up in his favourite chair and hid behind the curtains.

Flynn, when he returned home, is said to have removed his coat, nodded to Barrymore, taken a few steps towards his bar for a quick nightcap – frozen, refocused on the body on his chair and let out a blood-curdling scream.

'They hadn't embalmed him yet', the actor explained in his autobiography.

31 May

2002

A man from Chongqing in western China was taken to hospital after trying to imitate Mary Poppins. According to the *South China Morning Post*, the man became alarmed when his microwave started acting strangely and appeared to be about to explode. Naturally he decided to leap from the window of his second-floor apartment using an umbrella as a parachute, thinking that it would help him to float to the ground just like in the popular musical film. He sustained two broken legs after discovering the hard truth about gravity and reality.

June

1 June

1996

When a radio reporter in the small Philippines city of Lucena announced that he had just heard news that the nearby volcano Mount Banahaw was about to blow its top for the first time since 1743, residents were understandably alarmed. The only thing that actually erupted, however, was panic, as thousands left their homes and two people died of heart attacks. The DJ had been fooled by hoaxers.

2 June

1995

A golfer in Wales was astonished when his tee shot went straight up a sheep's backside. Peter Croke, who was playing with friends at the Southerndown Golf Club, near Porthcawl, said, 'The sheep looked mildly surprised by the whole thing but we were in hysterics'.

And while the sheep may not have been particularly pleased, the strange event was of considerable benefit to Mr Croke, since the animal then moved the ball 30 metres closer to his original target.

'The sheep walked off toward the 17th hole and then seemed to shake the ball free like laying an egg', explained Croke, who went on to win the match.

1897

Mark Twain's obituary was published, somewhat prematurely. 'The report of my death was an exaggeration', said the writer after reading it.

3 June

2004

Paul McKenna received a text message from his girlfriend Liz Fuller asking him to watch her appearance on TV show *Auction World* on this afternoon. During a sale of engagement rings Fuller looked into the camera, informed the public that McKenna was 'emotionally inadequate' and told him that she was leaving him. As she closed the bidding on the next item, she declared it was 'Going, going, gone . . . just like Paul'.

Not to be outdone, McKenna later told reporters that he found the stunt 'hilarious' and added: 'We only went out for a couple of months and the break-up has been more significant than the relationship.'

4 June

1974

To help increase their ticket sales the American baseball team the Cleveland Indians today held a beer promotion for their match against the Texas Rangers. The offer was that for 10 cents apiece fans could drink as much Stroh's beer as they could manage. Perhaps unsurprisingly, the crowd ended up drinking rather a lot.

The first sign that general alcohol consumption may have been excessive came early on in the game, when a woman ran out on to the field and lifted her skirt. She was followed soon afterwards by a naked man who sprinted to second base just as a player hit a home run. Not to be outdone, a father and his son then ran out to the field, lowered their trousers and mooned the by now baying fans. Soon the players on the field found themselves the target of hot dogs, beer cans and, most alarmingly, an empty gallon jug of Thunderbird wine.

Matters came to a head when a member of the crowd stole the glove and cap from a member of the away team. The player reacted angrily and was soon joined by every other member of the Texas Rangers, all wielding their baseball bats. The crowd in turn picked up stadium seats and whatever other objects came to hand and started a slow advance. The Cleveland Indians quickly joined the mêlée, also bearing bats on the side of the team who had been their opponents moments earlier.

Not surprisingly, the game was at this stage called off, but not before fans had grabbed all the bases on the pitch as souvenirs and torn up many of the seats in the stadium. The president of the American baseball League, Lee McPhail, commented perceptively that 'there was no question that beer played a part in the riot'. Next time there was a beer promotion, fans were allowed a maximum of four glasses.

5 June

2003

'All I said to the owner was that it wasn't good enough and we weren't happy with the service', said Pierluigi Lanzoni, a guest at the Villa Pinuccia, a hotel near Naples. 'The next thing he was shouting he'd had enough and then he locked the doors.'

According to reports, owner Anello Aiello's exact words after receiving a torrent of complaints from his guests about bad food, poor service, unchanged sheets and dirty bathrooms were: 'Right. That's it. I've had enough. No one is leaving!'

He then locked the doors of the dining-room, where eighty angry guests were eating their singularly unsatisfactory meal. He was only persuaded to open them again when the police came and arrested him.

6 June

2002

A wedding on top of icy Mount Ranier in Washington State had to be called off when the bride, groom and minister were blown into a crevasse by a gust of wind. The three were rescued by helicopter, and the ceremony was successfully completed in hospital, only slightly hampered by the fact that the bride's leg was in a cast.

1761

The transit of Venus was one of the great astronomical events of the eighteenth century. In 1761 star-gazers travelled to observatories all over the world, hoping to measure it because (following a discovery by Edmund Halley) they thought that by recording how long it took Venus to progress across the face of the sun, they could work out how far the fiery orb was from the earth. These journeys were often made through war and considerable hardship, and the successful measurement of the transit is regarded as one of the greatest scientific feats in history.

Not all of the astronomers met with success, however. Guillaume Le Gentil, for instance, had set out from Paris a year before the rare event, attempting to get to Pondicherry in India. Annoyingly for the industrious Frenchman, when he arrived, he found that the British were besieging the town and there was no way he could land there. On the big day of 6 June he was forced to take his measurements from the deck of a ship, which heaved and rolled so much that his recordings were useless.

That only marked the start of his bad luck. Knowing that Venus would move across the sun in another eight years (transits occur in pairs separated by eight years, with 120 years between each cycle), he decided to stay in the area. In 1768 he was able not only to land in Pondicherry but also to set up a fully equipped observatory. All went perfectly until the day of the transit, when clouds obscured the sun, and Guillaume again recorded nothing. 'I was more than two weeks in singular dejection', he wrote in his journal, little knowing that yet worse was to come. When he eventually arrived home, he discovered that he had been declared dead, his wife had remarried, all his possessions had been distributed among his heirs . . . Oh, and he'd lost his job at the Royal Academy of Sciences.

7 June

1971

'I am so healthy that I expect to live on and on', proclaimed J.I. Rodale, the publisher of *Prevention* magazine and an early advocate of organic farming, during a recording of the *Dick Cavett Show* in the USA. A few minutes later, while Cavett was speaking to journalist Pete Hamill, he returned to Rodale, who appeared to be snoring, to ask him, 'Are we boring you?' Rodale had just had a heart attack and died.

8 June

1999

Tawana Dawson, a fifteen-year-old girl, was expelled from Pensacola High School in Florida for being in possession of a dangerous weapon: a pair of nail clippers.

A teacher spotted Miss Dawson's clippers on the desk of another pupil, who had borrowed them to clean her nails, and realized that its two-inch knife attachment contravened the school's zero tolerance on weapons policy.

Miss Dawson's explanation that she thought the attachment was simply for cleaning fingernails was disregarded.

9 June

1980

Comedy genius Richard Pryor had an accident while freebasing on cocaine. The first indication that anyone else had that something had gone wrong was when Pryor burst out of his house, covered in flames. Fortunately, he survived the incident. He was later even able to view the whole episode philosophically, noting that 'when you're running down the street on fire, people get out of your way'. He also observed that 'Fire is inspirational. They should use it in the Olympics, because I ran the 100 in 4.3.'

10 June

2005

When police rushed into Jabulani Siphethu's small village house in the Tugela Ferry area of South Africa, they found him stark naked and attempting to dispose of his wife's body by eating it. This misguided effort backfired horribly – and the wife was granted revenge from beyond the grave – when Siphethu proceeded to choke on the portion of his wife's face he had been chewing and promptly died in front of the alarmed police officers.

11 June

2006

When Shirley Hatcher parked her car in North Road, Southampton, and went off to the hairdresser, there were no restrictions in place. When she got back, however, contractors had painted a disabled bay around her vehicle – and she had been whacked with a £60 fine. To add injury to insult, the car was also covered with spots of paint. Southampton Council eventually apologized, dropped the fine and promised to pay for repairs to the car. 'Occasionally things go wrong, no matter how hard we try to get things right', said a philosophical spokeswoman for the council, neatly summing up one of the fundamental problems of life itself.

12 June

1999

Today an unidentified Russian put into action a very innovative, very illegal and not particularly smart plan to catch lots of fish. He connected a long extension cord to the mains power supply in his house and ran it down to a nearby river. The first part of the plan worked very well. The fish were shocked, died and floated to the surface. A lack of foresight ruined the second section, however. The man neglected to unplug the power before wading into the water, and his instant death prevented him from being able to retrieve his catch.

13 June

1993

Seventy-year-old Armando Pinelli won an argument with a friend over who got to sit on the one chair under the shade of a palm tree in Foggia, Italy, but his victory turned out to be Pyrrhic. Shortly after he sat down, the tree fell over and killed him.

14 June

2006

George W. Bush was having a difficult day even by his own standards. Problems started when he said, 'I think – tide turning – see, as I remember – I was raised in the desert, but tides kind of – it's easy to see a tide turn – did I say those words?' He took gaffe-making into new, previously unexplored territory, however, when he entered into the following exchange with Peter Wallsten of the *Los Angeles Times*:

> *President Bush*: Peter. Are you going to ask that question with shades on?
> *Wallsten*: I can take them off.
> *Bush*: I'm interested in the shade look, seriously.
> *Wallsten*: All right, I'll keep it, then.
> *Bush*: For the viewers, there's no sun.
> *Wallsten*: I guess it depends on your perspective.
> *Bush*: Touché.

Peter Wallsten is legally blind. Bush was later made to apologize, having being informed of his condition.

15 June

1992

Dan Quayle, then the US Republican Vice-President and widely believed to be a bit of a chump, was in Trenton, New Jersey, hoping to improve his image with some feel-good public relations. He was going to help out at a high school spelling competition, which was naturally being staged in front of television cameras.

The first child to have to spell a word was twelve-year-old William Figueroa, who carefully and correctly wrote out the word 'Potato' on a blackboard.

'You're close,' Quayle told him in a gentle voice, 'but you left a little something off. The "e" off the end. Think of "potatoe", how's it spelled. You're right phonetically, but what else? There ya go . . . all right!' The image of the polite boy dutifully adding the erroneous 'e' was broadcast around the world.

Commenting on the incident, Figueroa said that it made him think that Quayle was as much of an 'idiot' as everyone had always said. 'I knew he was wrong, but since he's the Vice-President I went back to the blackboard and put an "e" on the end and went back to my seat', he explained the following night, when invited on to the *David Letterman Show*. 'Afterward, I went to the dictionary, and there was potato like I spelled it.'

Quayle himself described the infamous 'potatoe incident' in his autobiography as 'a defining moment of the worst kind imaginable'.

16 June

1998

When 51-year-old Chad Bibbings's wife left him for a younger man, his thoughts turned quickly to revenge. 'She's very prim,' he said later, 'so I decided to tape the two of them having sex, and then send the recording to all her friends.'

Initially, the plan went smoothly. He successfully gained entry to his ex-wife's house and positioned himself under the bed to await the couple's return. Upsettingly for Mr Bibbings, however, his wife and her new lover's amours were so passionate that the bottom of the bed began to slam into him repeatedly, ramming the springs into his face with a power which the cuckolded husband likened to 'Mike Tyson's fist'.

Soon he decided that he could take no more and was forced to call out for help. Mrs Bibbings's lover admitted that his initial thought upon discovering Mr Bibbings under his bed was to punch him in the face, but when he saw the condition he was in already he said, 'I just called an ambulance'.

17 June

2002

By all accounts, jails in Costa Rica are particularly unpleasant and notoriously hard to break out of. Considerable kudos therefore goes to Oswaldo Hernández, a 28-year-old Panamanian accused of killing a judge (in itself a fairly big mistake), who managed to evade his captors and flee into the dense jungle that lies between Costa Rica and Panama.

His achievement was considerably undermined, however, when he was eaten by a crocodile as he attempted to swim to freedom.

1933

In Kansas City friends of Frank Nash gunned down the four FBI agents who were escorting the notorious gangster to prison. Their plan went awry, however, because Nash himself was caught up in the rain of bullets and also died.

1815

On the eve of the Battle of Waterloo, Napoleon was in confident mood. 'Wellington is a bad general, the English are bad soldiers: we will settle the matter by lunchtime.'

The battle actually finished at dusk, with the total rout of Napoleon's army.

18 June

1998

A taxi driver from Helsinki in Finland today received a ten-month sentence for offloading a drunken passenger into a rubbish tip.

'The client changed his mind many times during the long drive and urinated on the seat. The taxi driver got annoyed with him and drove him to the dump', explained judge Tarja Solaja. The driver's solution was to drive his unruly passenger to the local rubbish dump and dispose of him there. He was left among the garbage in freezing January temperatures until the police came and rescued him, having been alerted by a refuse worker who saw the driver pushing him out of his taxi.

The driver admitted in court that he may have acted 'rather heedlessly'.

1815

During the Battle of Waterloo the Duke of Wellington's companion Lord Uxbridge was surprised when a cannon ball smashed into his right knee. He was, however, determined not to betray the British stiff upper lip. 'By God sir! I've lost my leg', was his only complaint. 'By God sir, so you have', was Wellington's reply before calmly calling for stretcher-bearers.

19 June

2002

Because a Zurich insurance company doubted a chef's claim that his finger had been cut off in a meat slicer, they sent along an inspector to review the offending equipment. When he turned it on, it chopped his finger off too. The chef got his money.

20 June

2005

Tim Shaw, the British radio DJ, has had a career of many notable lows. He has forced pepper into his own eyes, electrocuted his own scrotum, bobbed for apples in his co-presenter's urine and faced suspension after he broke into his boss's house, scrawled the words 'Bell-End' over his kitchen and waited for him to return – live on air. Many thought Shaw's nadir must have surely come when he nearly died after choking on a U-shaped sausage, on which he was imitating oral sex. However, even this memorable moment was surpassed when his wife sold his £25,000 Lotus sports car for just 50p.

The incident occurred shortly after an interview in which Shaw informed British glamour model Jodie Marsh that he would be prepared to leave his wife and kids for her. His wife, who had been listening at home, was still smarting from an earlier incident in which the controversial DJ told listeners that he fantasized about his wife's sister while he was having sex. Not surprisingly, the DJ's enraged better half reacted angrily.

She quickly placed an advert for his black sports car on the online auction site eBay with the message: 'I need to get rid of this car immediately – ideally in the next three to four hours, before my cheating arsehole husband gets home to find it gone and all his belongings in the street.' She advertised it for 50p and clicked the 'Buy It Now' option, so that no higher bids were necessary. It was gone within five minutes.

Mrs Shaw said, 'The car is his pride and joy, but the idiot put my name on the log-book so I just sold it. I didn't care about the money, I just wanted to get him back.' The buyer, who asked to remain anonymous, later left some positive feedback on the site: 'Thank you, Hayley, the car is excellent. Thank your hubby for me too.'

21 June

1998

A man from Kentucky accidentally shot his best friend when he took him up on his dare to shoot a can off his head 'William Tell-style'. Witnesses told the police that the two men 'had been drinking' when Larry Slusher bet his childhood friend Silas Caldwell that he couldn't manage to shoot a beer can off the top of his head. Silas proved him correct by missing the can and blasting out his brains.

Caldwell fled the scene but soon gave himself up to police. Phlegmatic local sheriff Harold Harbin said, 'He gave us his gun and didn't give us any trouble. He was just drinking and acting like a fool, I guess.'

1999

'The only thing I know about Slovakia is what I learned first-hand from your foreign minister, who came to Texas', said George W. Bush, but his charm offensive with a Slovakian journalist turned out to be just offensive when it was realized that Bush had actually been visited by the Prime Minister of Slovenia.

22 June

1774

'On the 22nd of June 1774', starts Robert Chambers in his incomparable *Book of Days*, 'a man named John Day lost his life in a manner singularly exhibiting the great ignorance with respect to the simplest physical facts which prevailed at the period.'

Day, 'an ignorant but ingenious millwright', thought he had invented a diving machine. The only problem was that he neglected, as Chambers puts it, to provide for 'any communication with the air'. That's to say, there was no oxygen supply in his contraption.

What's more, Day couldn't think of any reason that a diving machine would be at all useful, other than the laying of bets relating to how long he could stay below the surface of the water. Accordingly, he entered into an arrangement with a shifty character known only as 'Blake', who agreed to put up the money for the building of the machine and pay Day 10 per cent of all the profits he would make from running the book on how long he could stay submerged.

'Day's plan, if it had no other merit, had that of simplicity', continues Chambers. 'His machine was merely a water-tight box, or compartment, attached to an old vessel by means of screws.' Day would be lowered into the water, equipped with a watch and a wax taper for light. When the agreed time was reached, he would undo the screws and simply float to the surface.

'Granting that a man could live . . . without a constant supply of fresh air, nothing could be easier than Day's proposed plan', says Chambers. The first stages certainly went well. The bets were collected, the diving box was made and successfully lowered, together with Day, his candle and watch, 132 feet beneath the surface of the water in Plymouth Sound . . . 'from whence neither it nor the unfortunate man ever arose'.

Interestingly, Chambers also tells us, a 'pretentious monthly periodical of the time, *The British Magazine of Arts, Sciences, and Literature*', gave an exhaustive list of the possible reasons for Day's failure, none of which alludes to the problem of a lack of 'fresh air'.

23 June

1993

John Wayne Bobbitt's peaceful night's sleep was interrupted when his wife, Lorena, chopped off a portion of his penis with a kitchen knife. Lorena then jumped into her car, carrying the severed bit of her husband's body – and chucked it out of the window as she tore off down the street. Miraculously, the police found the missing member and it was re-attached to John Wayne.

In her initial statements to the police Lorena explained that she'd been driven to schlong-slicing because her husband was 'selfish' and 'wouldn't give her an orgasm'. During the subsequent trial, however, it emerged that Lorena and John Wayne's was a particularly disastrous relationship and that Lorena's actions could largely be explained by the fact that her husband had been abusing her. She escaped the most serious charges and became something of a feminist *cause célèbre*. John Wayne and his restored manhood, meanwhile, went on to star in the porn films *Frankenpenis* and *John Wayne Bobbitt – Uncut*.

Interestingly, Bobbitt is also the name of an aquatic worm, so called because the female of the species often attacks the male's sex organ after mating, detaching it and then feeding it to her young.

24 June

1963

The Rolling Stones made their TV début on the British programme *Thank Your Lucky Stars*. 'The band's OK,' the show's producer advised Andrew Loog Oldham, manager of the group at the time, 'but if I were you, I'd get rid of that vile-looking singer with the tyre-tread lips.'

The Rolling Stones ignored his advice, kept Mick Jagger and went on to have a number of quite successful records.

25 June

1876

'Hurrah boys, we've got them! We'll finish them up and then go home to our station.' So said General Custer when first sighting an encampment of Sioux Indians just before the Battle of Little Big Horn, where he and his army were wiped off the face of the earth.

26 June

2005

A fourteen-year-old girl's quiet picnic with her family at a popular New Hampshire swimming hole took a turn for the strange when she visited a toilet and saw a 45-year-old man staring up at her.

The girl's family called the police, who came and found the man (the alarmingly named G.J. Moody) pressed up against the wall in the large cess-pit beneath the rudimentary toilets. He didn't say anything until ordered to come out.

Captain Jon Hebert, of the Carroll County Sheriff's Department, said firefighters then had to clean Moody down with their hoses before anyone could get close enough to handcuff him.

'We had to decontaminate him. We treated him as if he were hazardous material', Hebert told the local paper, the *Kennebec Journal*. 'I started this business in 1980, and I have never in my career encountered anybody in this type of situation.'

Moody later claimed that he had been looking for his lost wedding ring, which he said had fallen down the toilet when he was changing his clothes. He noted that he was in the Ladies because the Gents was busy. He declined to answer, however, when he was asked why he hadn't just alerted the park ranger to his loss. There was also no explanation of why he had been wearing waders.

1990

When he was campaigning for US President in 1988, George H. W. Bush said, 'The Congress will push me to raise taxes and I'll say no. And they'll push and I'll say no. And they'll push again and I'll say to them, "Read my lips, no new taxes".' The crowd watching the speech went crazy, as did the country, who duly elected him as their leader. On this day, he introduced new tax rises. 'We stand by everything that's ever been said', said his press secretary to dismiss reporters who were suggesting that the President had broken a campaign promise.

1284

One hundred and thirty children disappeared from the German town of Hamelin, and the legend of the Pied Piper was born.

27 June

1959

Back in the days of the draft in the USA, not all soldiers enjoyed their duties. Pfc Andrew God, for instance, was annoyed by the fact that he was made to peel potatoes in Fort Meyer, Virginia. He made such a bad job of it, and hacked at his spuds so brutally, that his mess sergeant reported him to his captain for disciplinary action, and God was ordered to perform two hours' hard labour every day for the next fortnight.

However, God, who had been an architect in Detroit before he was called up, was smarter than the average grunt, and knew that he was entitled to a court-martial before undergoing any punishment. The army was therefore compelled to take him to tribunal on the following grounds: Pfc Andrew God, twenty-five, 'having knowledge of a lawful order ... to peel and eye potatoes as directed, an order which it was his duty to obey, did . . . fail to obey the same. [He] did, without proper authority, wilfully suffer potatoes, of some value, military property of the U.S., to be destroyed by improper peeling.'

During the case God's mess sergeant gave a vivid demonstration of God's woeful peeling technique on a batch of potatoes, and it looked like things were going to go against the young private. However, his defence managed to argue that God was hampered by the fact that he had no peeler and was forced to use a knife. They were even able to prove that God's peelings (which had been saved as evidence by the company commander) weighed less than a similar batch by the sergeant. God's will prevailed, he got off scot-free at the end of the two-hour trial, and the army was left looking rather foolish.

When asked to explain the proceedings to the media, a military press officer conceded: 'The whole thing may seem ridiculous to someone outside the Army.'

28 June

1914

Serb nationalist Gavrilo Princip shot dead Archduke Franz Ferdinand of Austria and so lit the fuse that exploded into one of the bloodiest conflicts to afflict mankind: the First World War.

This momentous event might never have happened if the Archduke's driver hadn't taken a wrong turning, forcing him to reverse down a narrow street, in the process of which he stalled the car right outside the café where Princip, who had previously given up all hope of carrying out his assassination, had retired for a sandwich. The rest is history.

29 June

1914

Khioniya Guseva stabbed mad monk Grigori Rasputin in the chest and shouted, 'I have killed the anti-Christ'. She hadn't. He survived the attack, ran away and then beat her up when she attacked him again.

1509

The otherwise unsuccessful alchemist Abbot John Damien secured himself immortality (of a sort) when he declared that he was going to fly to France from Scotland. He had assistants build him a pair of wings and jumped from the walls of Stirling Castle. Onlookers who saw the proto-scientist's inevitable dramatic fall were surprised to hear his complaining voice emerging from the ground below. Damien's landing had been softened by the castle dung heap, and he escaped with only a few broken bones. His pride, meanwhile, was quickly restored by the bold declaration that his experiment had failed only because the wings had been made with feathers from chickens and that chickens weren't very good at flying. He never repeated the attempt, however.

30 June

1997

When Carlo Pampini, a 31-year-old Italian male stripper, entered a private suite in a Naples hotel to honour a hen party booking, he found the audience wasn't quite what he was expecting. 'They were older than usual,' he said, 'and very serious.'

In spite of this stony reception, Carlo, a true professional, had soon removed his clothes and wedged a large sausage between his buttocks. It was when he invited one woman to remove said meat product with her teeth that he was hit with the first chair. After that the onslaught began. More and more of the old women piled in, laying into him with chairs and handbags, leaving him senseless on the floor.

When he came round, he was informed that he'd made a crucial error with room numbers. Instead of a hen party, he'd taken it upon himself to entertain a meeting of the Catholic Mothers against Pornography Guild.

July

1 July

2003

In the First Baptist Church in the small town of Forest, Ohio, a travelling preacher, Ron Hardman, was quite literally talking up a storm as thunder crashed outside the building. He told the quaking congregation that the sound was God's voice. 'That's right, God, we hear you', he cried and looked heavenward. Then lightning hit the church.

'It was awesome, just awesome', said church member Ronnie Cheney, who was in the building when the strike hit. 'You could hear the storm building outside . . . he just kept asking God what else he needed to say. He was asking for a sign and he got one.'

The bolt initially struck the steeple and then channelled in through Harman's clip-on microphone. Witnesses said there was a blue aura, the lights flickered on and off and the church's sound system exploded. Mr Hardman, however, was unharmed and carried on preaching for another twenty minutes – until the congregation realized that the church was on fire and fled in panic.

Tiles from the church roof smashed a car to pieces in the car park, the steeple was destroyed and repairs to the church were estimated at $20,000.

2 July

1982

Larry Walters had always wanted to fly, but bad eyesight had prevented him from fulfilling his dream of becoming a pilot. Even so, on 2 July 1982 he managed to realize his ambition by tying forty-five helium-filled weather balloons to a garden chair and taking off from the garden of his girlfriend's house in Long Beach, California.

He thought that his flying chair would level out at around 100 feet, and then he'd be able to lower it by shooting at the balloons with an airgun he'd packed for the purpose. Once in the air, however, he became afraid that shooting the balloons would desta-bilize the chair and tip him to the ground. What's more, it kept on rising and drifted into the approach zone for nearby Long Beach airport. Walters climbed to an impressive 16,000 feet while aero-planes zoomed above, below and beside him.

Eventually he steeled himself to shoot a few balloons. His chair slowly drifted down, finally coming to an undignified halt when the balloon cables became hopelessly entangled in power lines. Walters jumped down the remaining distance to the ground – and was immediately arrested by waiting members of the LAPD. When reporters asked why he'd done such an unusual thing, he replied, 'A man can't just sit around'.

2001

Susan Mary Aris, a British woman, died in Athens when a bomb she was carrying in her car was set off by her pet dog. On the day of her untimely death, she had been on the way to avenge the killing of two leading members of her surrogate family, a notorious Greek crime ring. The bomb was stashed under the handbrake of her car, and the remote control was in her handbag. Her plan was foiled shortly after she pulled out of her home, however, when her pet Rottweiler, Boris, accidentally sat on the explosives and detonated them. Sadly, Boris did not survive the blast either.

3 July

1939

The San Francisco Golden Gate Exposition was a huge fair put together to celebrate the building of the world's largest suspension bridge at the time: the famous Golden Gate Bridge itself. It featured huge sculpture parks, displays of rare plants, stunning architectural displays and, of course, gigantic fair rides. Circling above these fair rides at 800 feet was the famous Goodyear blimp, an airship with the name of the tyre manufacturer printed on its side.

When Left O'Doul, the manager of the San Francisco Seals baseball club, spotted this giant balloon, he decided it might amuse the crowd to see one of his players catch a ball from its great height. Accordingly, he arranged for a ball to be dropped from the balloon over the pitch when his players were gathered to play a match on the evening of 3 July.

Only one player, Joe 'Mule' Sprinz, had agreed to take part in his manager's bizarre scheme and stood plum in the middle of the field as the ball was dropped from above his head.

Once dropped, the ball accelerated at a terrifying 10 metres per second, reaching a terminal velocity of around 95 m.p.h. Sprinz missed the first and second balls, which pounded the turf. For the third, however, he positioned himself just right and caught the ball cleanly in his glove.

He took up the story from his hospital bed. 'I saw it all the way,' he explained, 'but it looked about the size of an aspirin tablet.'

The ball was moving so fast it slammed the gloved hand into his face, much to the alarm of the crowd. He fractured his jaw and lost five of his teeth, and his face was cut to shreds. Worse still, historical opinion is divided as to whether he actually took the catch, and many contemporaries declared they saw the ball rolling away as Sprinz himself rolled on the floor in agony.

4 July

2001

Ethem Sahin's quiet Wednesday afternoon game of dominoes in a Turkish coffee house was rudely interrupted when a cow fell through the roof and landed him in hospital.

When Sahin first came round and his friends told him what had happened, he thought they were pulling his (broken) leg. 'I couldn't believe it', he told the local news agency. But it was true. Apparently the cow had been grazing on the side of the hill that the coffee shop was built into and had wandered on to its roof, before crashing through on to Mr Sahin. Sahin needed stitches in his head as well as several weeks with his damaged leg in plaster. The animal was unhurt.

1826

Fifty years to the day after the signing of the Declaration of Independence John Adams, one of the driving forces behind the historical document, died. His last words were jubilant: 'Thomas Jefferson still survives', he cried happily. Actually, his co-signer had passed away several hours earlier that same day.

1776

'Nothing of importance happened today', wrote George III of England, unaware that across the Atlantic the Declaration of Independence had just been signed and that his country was about to lose the American colonies.

5 July

2002

Stingo Jones, a popular figure on the English festival circuit, was driving through France on the way to a party in Italy. The long drive, undertaken in a rusting old van, took him through several small villages. In one of these villages he was just passing an old lady walking her pet dog when the animal jumped out in front of his vehicle and he smashed into it.

Jumping down, he was confronted with the sight of the dog twitching on the ground and an understandably distraught French granny. He tried to apologize to her, but she spoke no English and he spoke no French. He did understand, however, thanks to her manic gesturing, that she wanted him to put her pet out of its misery. So he went and got the spade from the back of his van, gritted his teeth and whacked the twitching dog over the back of the head.

The poor animal finally lay still. He tried to speak to the woman again, and again made no progress. In a flurry of misunderstood apologies and fruitless hand-waving he got back into his van and drove on to Italy.

A few days later, once the festival was finished, Stingo's route took him back through the same village. There he was surprised to see the same old woman walking slowly down the street. He was then horrified to note that she was walking the exact same dog. It appeared to be entirely unharmed; apart from the huge bandage wrapped around its head where he had battered it with the spade. This time he didn't get out of his van.

6 July

1994

Scott Kell, a karate brown belt, often practised his kicks and chops in his tenth-floor flat in Salford. Sadly, on this day in 1994 he forgot to close the window and an over-enthusiastic high kick sent him hurtling to his death.

7 July

2003

A group of teenagers in Nova Scotia made the most of some fine summer weather to get up to no good. They stole a boat and took it out to sea under cover of darkness, found a nice quiet beach, burned their vessel to cover up their crime and partied the night away. It was only when dawn broke that they realized that they had landed on an uninhabited island and destroyed their only means of escape. They were rescued by helicopter and then charged with theft.

8 July

1998

A bridegroom in India showed up to his wedding so drunk that his bride called the police and had him arrested. The *Hindustan Times* reported that the man was dragged away from his own reception in Hapur, New Delhi, shouting drunken insults at the guests. Fortunately all was not lost, as one of the man's neighbours gallantly proposed to the bride after she and her parents called off the wedding and she married him that very night. The jilted groom was later released and returned home single and nursing a sore head.

9 July

1993

Garry Hoy, a 39-year-old lawyer, was said to be one of the 'best and brightest' of his prestigious 200-strong firm based in a towering skyscraper in downtown Toronto. So it was especially sad when he tried to demonstrate the safety of his office's windows to visiting law students by running into it with his shoulder, crashed through the pane of glass and fell twenty-four floors to his death.

10 July

2004

An attempt to break the fire-walking world record – and incidentally raise some money for charity – got off to a good start when
no fewer than 341 people turned up to walk across hot coals in
Dunedin, New Zealand.

No fewer than twenty-eight people had to be treated for serious
burns, however, and eleven of them had to be rushed to hospital.
Their medical bills amounted to far more than the £350 they raised
for charity in the first place.

Just to rub salt into their blisters and burns, a spokeswoman
from the *Guinness Book of Records* then informed the organizers
that the fire-walking record is based on distance, not the number of
people taking part.

11 July

2004

Footage of a thief lowering himself by a rope into their gallery
in full view of all the cameras was amusing enough for security
guards at the Saper galleries in Michigan. However, the funniest moments came when he attempted to climb back out again –
and realized that he couldn't. There was no way out of the
locked doors either. The next bit of film showed him using the
gallery's own phone to call the police so they could come and
rescue him.

The injury to the would-be robber's pride can't have been eased
when gallery owner Roy Saper commented to the *Michigan State
News*: 'There are professional thieves, but this guy was not only
not a professional, he wasn't even an apprentice – he was a total
loser . . . and he could have waited until we opened at 1 p.m.'

12 July

1995

'Bruce Jensen is just incredibly naïve', said prosecutor Bill McGuire. 'You've got a situation here where love is unbelievably blind.' Jensen's three-and-a-half-year marriage had just come to a dramatic end. He'd discovered that not only had his bride defrauded him of almost $60,000, but that 'she' was a he.

The devout Mormon Jensen had 'married' Felix Urioste – or Leasa Bibianna Herrera, as he was calling himself at that time – after just one sexual encounter. Urioste, who was then masquerading as a female doctor under a Cleopatra-style wig and heavy make-up, had told Jensen that he was pregnant with twins after their (fully clothed) night of passion, and Jensen had felt obliged to marry him. Shortly afterwards Urioste told Jensen that the twins had been stillborn and that he was suffering from cancer. The marriage survived these traumatic events but remained celibate from then on. Even the fact that Urioste grew a moustache didn't alert the sheltered Jensen, who later explained to reporters that his mother had been able to grow one too.

The imposture was finally exposed after Urioste ran away in April 1995 – with a number of Jensen's credit cards. Jensen had filed a missing person's report, and the name he gave for Urioste (Leasa Herrera) matched one of the nineteen that police found on Urioste's person when they arrested him for speeding in Nevada early in July.

When he discovered the awful truth, Jensen sought an annulment of the marriage, citing 'irreconcilable differences'. He told reporters that he planned to return to his home in Wyoming and 'crawl in a hole for a few years and not let anyone within rifle range'.

13 July

2003

A guest at the Capri Motel in Kansas had been exactly right to say that his room smelt like something had died in it. The proof was the body of a man clad in fishnet stockings and a woman's headscarf that was found under his bed.

The guest had been complaining about the smell for the past three days, but the motel's management had told him that nothing could be done about it and that the room had already been cleaned. He eventually checked out, saying he could no longer tolerate the smell. Cleaning staff then discovered the body (which had been obscured from view by the wooden panels around the base of the bed) when they lifted up a mattress.

The policeman who came to the scene, Sergeant Darin Snapp, told the press that the Capri had been closed several times before for 'indecency and poor hygiene' and probably would be again soon. On the other hand, he dryly noted, 'it is a competitively priced motel, with many facilities including a pool and a gym'.

1951

The composer Arnold Schoenberg's fear of the number 13 was proved well grounded when he died on this Friday 13th, aged seventy-six (a significant number because, as he obsessively repeated to all around him, 7 + 6 = 13, a sure sign that his end was imminent). According to legend, his wife leaned over to him at 13 minutes to midnight and whispered, 'You see, the day is almost over. All that worry was for nothing.' He looked at her and died.

14 July

1998

Frank Sytner and his wife, Elizabeth, today lost a court case and were forced to accept that mud is a part of countryside living.

Sytner was a millionaire who had made his fortune selling BMWs and was eager to get away from it all and embrace the quiet life. Far from being quiet, however, Sytner was alarmed to discover that the countryside could often be dirty and was full of sheep.

He was especially annoyed at a neighbouring farmer who had let these inconvenient animals on to the road at lambing time, so he tried to sue him for making a mess of the road. Mr Sytner said, 'I went to have a look at the track and saw a large number of sheep. I counted eighteen. There was an unbelievable amount of mud. It was impassable.'

Mrs Sytner, meanwhile, was equally dissatisfied. She had been troubled by cows. 'I was in my garden and heard cows making a noise in the field. It was annoying, so I went to see what was happening', she told the judge. When he put it to her that it might be normal to hear cows in the countryside, she replied: 'Yes, it's unfortunate, isn't it?'

The judge threw out the case, taking the not unreasonable view that on a country road 'mud was inevitable'.

15 July

1995

Many Hindus consider 15 July an inauspicious date. It's thought that the best way to ward off the bad luck caused by the day's bad astrology is to visit the right shrine and pray hard.

It's difficult to say whether the events in 1995 proved worshippers right or wrong. What is certain is that lots of people were killed in stampedes. At one holy site some fifty-eight unfortunates died when they were crushed or impaled on a bamboo security fence. Another fifteen met their end in a mêlée on a narrow bridge near a Shiva temple in Haridwar on the Ganges.

16 July

1966

Undertaker Harold Ingrams was at work embalming a body when it woke up from a deep coma – and beat him up. 'None of my friends in the funeral business has ever had anything like this happen', complained the traumatised Ingrams to reporters visiting him in hospital.

17 July

2002

A policeman patrolling Regent's Canal towpath in Camden, north London, made an unexpected drugs bust when he playfully squeezed the horn on a bike of a man to whom he was chatting and a bag of cannabis flew out.

1994

A herd of sheep committed mass suicide in a lake in Inner Mongolia. Two animals jumped into the water initially, and then 249 followed them in spite of desperate attempts by their shepherd to stop them. Vets had no explanation for this extraordinary behaviour.

18 July

2002

Matthew Cooper was just falling asleep at 2 a.m. in his relatives' house in Gainesville, Florida, when he heard a car alarm go off. Being an all-American hero, he grabbed his shotgun and ran outside in his boxers to tackle the intruder.

When he realized it was a neighbour's alarm rather than his, however, Cooper calmed down. His anger quickly turned to amusement when he spotted someone struggling inside the vehicle, trying to kick out the windows from the inside. Cooper went back to his house and alerted the police.

The man inside the car was David Christopher Lander, and he was stuck. When he'd broken in, he'd triggered an anti-theft device that locked all the doors – hence his vain attempts to smash his way out through the window.

By the time that the police arrived, spokesman Sergeant Keith Faulk said that Lander was 'all scrunched up' on the back seat. 'I guess he thought that the deputies couldn't seen him.'

Faulk went on to explain that, if Lander had just pushed a button on the driver's door, the locks would have been released and he'd have been able to escape. The spokesman also noted that for all his years on the force he had never seen anything so ridiculous, 'not where the suspect was caught because of his own ignorance. Maybe he needs a new line of work', he added. 'He's not very good at what he's doing now.'

19 July

1993

Vicki Jo Daily wasn't to blame for killing a man in February 1993. The police completely exonerated her, believing her explanation that the 56-year-old victim's snowmobile had stalled in front of her car and she was powerless to stop her pick-up truck from smashing into his vehicle.

In spite of all this, the dead man's widow was surprised when Ms Daily today filed a lawsuit against her husband's estate, citing the 'grave and crippling psychological injuries' she suffered 'by watching the man die'. Lawyers acting for Ms Daily said she expected significant financial compensation.

20 July

1984

Jim Fixx was convinced that running could not only improve your life; it could also lengthen it. When he took up the sport in 1968, aged thirty-five, he was overweight and smoked two packets of cigarettes a day. Within ten years he had transformed himself into a lithe, smoke-free athlete whose muscular legs graced the cover of the book he wrote to promote the benefits of his favourite pastime: *The Complete Book of Running*.

The book went on to sell more than a million copies, making it the best selling non-fiction book of its era. Sales took a severe dent after this fateful day in 1984, however, because Fixx suffered a massive heart attack while out on his daily run and died at the age of just fifty-two.

21 July

1999

Lee Hosken actually carried out his robbery fairly successfully, using a screwdriver to break into one Mathew Holden's Vauxhall Astra and taking off for a joyride with his girlfriend in tow.

His trouble started when he crashed the car and abandoned it. The fact that he left his fingerprints all over the wreck was helpful enough to the police, but Hosken's most astounding accomplishment was to have asked his girlfriend to take pictures of himself, screwdriver in hand, with a camera that he found in the car . . . and then to have left the camera behind in the glove compartment.

After he recovered his camera, Mr Holden was astonished when he took the film to be developed and saw Lee Hosken's mug grinning out at him. 'I was looking through the pictures when suddenly I saw my car and some bloke in it with a screwdriver in his hand. When I showed the police they recognized him straight away', he said. So it was that Hosken was sentenced to a two-year driving ban and two years' probation on this day in 1999.

His solicitor, Robin Shellard, told Bristol Crown Court, 'If there is one thing that runs through his life it's sheer idiocy.' A police wit, meanwhile, said, 'We are very grateful to this man for making his own arrest so easy. He quite literally put himself in the frame for his own crime.'

22 July

1991

Michael Kluznick was killed by an arrow shot from the bow of his friend Marc Kienkowski following a dispute over a game of Monopoly. During the subsequent court case a Pennsylvania District Attorney explained that the reason that Kienkowski was driven to take such drastic action was that 'he wanted to be the car rather than the thimble or the hat'.

23 July

1983

When Air Canada changed from imperial measurements to metric in 1983, one of the unforeseen consequences was a nearly fatal miscalculation in the fuel needed for a new Boeing 767 to fly from Montreal to Edmonton.

When an indicator warned the pilots that there was a fuel pressure problem on the plane's left side, they decided to divert to Winnipeg airport and changed course. It was a sensible decision because, soon afterwards, the left engine fell dead. Seconds later the right-side engine stopped as well. The 767 lost all power, and everything suddenly fell quiet – so quiet that the cockpit voice-recorder could easily pick out the words 'Oh fuck!'

Fortunately one of the pilots knew that there was an old air force base in the area and decided to try and glide the plane on to the landing ground there. Unfortunately, the base had recently become a public aerodrome, and the runway had been given over to drag-racing. On this day the whole place was crammed with cars and campers for a special 'family day', and a race was taking part on the runway.

Miraculously, the pilot managed to guide the plane in safely. The passengers suffered only a few minor injuries and the gathered sports car enthusiasts quickly put out the fire that started in the plane's nose cone.

Air Canada immediately sent a team of mechanics out from Winnipeg to look the plane over. On the way to the base their car ran out of fuel too. Another one had to be sent to pick them up.

1923

'Don't let it end like this', begged Mexican revolutionary Pancho Villa, seconds before dying from an assassin's bullet. 'Tell them I said something.'

24 July

1621

The Archbishop of Canterbury, George Abbott, started a long and noble tradition of important statesmen accidentally shooting underlings on hunting expeditions when he killed a gamekeeper, Peter Hawkins, with a loose arrow. A coroner favourable to the powerful bishop recorded a verdict of 'death by misadventure and his own fault' for the poor Hawkins. However, Abbott's many enemies never let him forget the incident, their zeal at reminding him fired by actions such as his decision to send 140 Oxford undergraduates to prison for failing to remove their hats in his presence and his habit of branding his enemies – on the face.

25 July

2005

A couple's passionate lovemaking was interrupted when two lifeboat teams arrived to 'rescue' them from the dinghy they were floating in. The couple had been making the most of a sunny morning just off the coast near Exeter when a walker on the shore heard their screams and thrashings. Fearing the worst, he alerted emergency services. The mistake was only realized when the two lifeboats reached the dinghy . . .

'I've never seen anything quite like it in all my eighteen years I've been doing the job', said lifeboat man Nigel Crang. 'I've never seen such things in a six-foot inflatable at such an early hour.'

Mr Crang also noted that the naked pair were 'a bit surprised when we turned up'.

26 July

2005

At first Ednor Rodrigues tried to deny stealing seven toothbrushes from a supermarket from Ribereiro Preto in Brazil. After all, as he was easily able to demonstrate to police by opening his mouth, he had no teeth at all. Eventually, however, when shown compelling CCTV evidence he confessed. 'I don't know why I did it', he said. 'I know it is a stupid thing . . . I have no teeth. What was I thinking?'

27 July

1575

The English nobleman Edward De Vere, Earl of Oxford, embarked on a long journey across Europe. According to the writer John Aubrey, these wanderings were prompted by a most unfortunate incident at court: 'This Earle of Oxford, making of his low obeisance to Queen Elizabeth, happened to let a Fart, at which he was so abashed and ashamed that he went to Travell, 7 years.'

When he returned, it became clear that the Queen had actually rather enjoyed his embarrassment. 'My lord,' she told him playfully when she welcomed him home, 'I had forgot the Fart.'

28 July

1998

Adam Gotz was absolutely convinced that the dead get resurrected. He termed himself a 'spiritual psychiatrist' and explained that the pyramids at Giza provided spiritual energy to enable believers to transcend humanity. Annoyingly, however, his friend Sarah Klimer showed some doubt about his Pharaonic beliefs. So when the two were on the rooftop bar of the 190-metre Cairo tower, in view of the pyramids that Gotz believed were going to bring him back to life, he took advantage of the low height of a safety barrier to throw himself over the edge of the building. He didn't come back.

29 July

2001

Thomas Rathbone and his young accomplice's attempt to rob a shop was severely hampered by the fact that the pair had forgotten to cut eye-holes into their masks. Shortly after they donned their unsuitable headwear, the pair were filmed on security cameras repeatedly bumping into each other and then demanding money from the wall of the shop. They were also completely oblivious to the fact that their newsagent victim was dialling 999.

They finally found the shop counter when they crashed into it, but this collision was the last straw for the teenagers, who then tore off their masks in frustration – right in front of the unblinking eye of a security camera.

Eventually they made off with just three packets of cigarettes before being quickly arrested by North Yorkshire police.

30 July

1937

The life of the infamous 'Prostitutes' Padre', Harold Davidson, was cut short when he was mauled by Freddy the lion at Skegness Zoo. Davidson, a Church of England vicar who had become notorious for the rather too close attention he paid to what he termed 'fallen women', had taken a job at the zoo, appearing alongside Freddy, to whom he read excerpts from the Bible. The lion was normally completely docile and generally fed by an eight-year-old girl, showing that he had a violent side only when he so fatally took against the naughty vicar. The audience reportedly thought it was part of the act and roared with laughter.

31 July

1995

A chicken fell down a 70-foot well in Nazlet Imara, an Egyptian village south of Cairo. Although not in itself remarkable, this event became so when eighteen-year-old Allam Sabet Al-Sayyed climbed down the well to rescue the stricken animal. Before he could reach it, a strong undercurrent in the well pulled him down and drowned him. Anxious about Allam's long absence, his elder brother also climbed down the well to investigate. He drowned too – as did another younger brother, Ahmad, then their fourteen-year-old sister Zeinab and then two elderly cousins, who had come to help.

The bodies of all six family members were later dragged up from their watery grave, along with the chicken, which had survived unscathed.

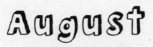

1 August

2006

Water was spouting from a statue in Pope John Paul II's home town, Wadowice. It must be, decided fervent local Catholics, the work of the recently deceased pontiff himself. This event was the sign from heaven that they had been waiting for!

Thousands of the faithful began flocking to the small Polish town to witness the incredible event, and to fill up whatever containers they could lay their hands on with the magic liquid from the 'miracle fountain'.

The pilgrims were no doubt very disappointed when the local mayor today told them that the cause of the new flow of water was nothing more special than a pipe that the council had installed beneath the statue. 'We didn't mean anything by it', she said apologetically. 'It was just supposed to make the statue look prettier.'

2 August

1970

Today the disastrous Powder Ridge Music Festival finally ended. Several things had gone awry at this long hot weekend at the wrong end of the 1960s, but the most notable oversight, as far as most attendees were concerned, was the almost total lack of music.

A stellar line-up including Janis Joplin, Sly and the Family Stone, Van Morrison and Fleetwood Mac had been promised, but, owing to a court injunction against the event gained by local residents, not one of the bands was allowed to play. An estimated 30,000 festival-goers had turned up anyway, hoping to make the most of their $20 tickets, but very soon boredom kicked in.

'It all goes to show that you can have a rock music festival without rock music', a member of the audience told reporters, somewhat optimistically; but events were to prove him wrong. The youths 'had nothing else to do', said Dr William Abruzzi, the on-site medic, 'other than take vast quantities of drugs', many of which were poor-quality, particularly a nasty brand of acid laced with strychnine.

LIFE magazine explained: 'The kids, deprived of the distraction of music, made it a festival of boredom, drugs, sex and nudity. So the townspeople had their public nuisance anyway.' Soon the local swimming hole, Powder Pond, had been polluted, and swimmers were falling sick; police helicopters spiralling overhead increased the sense of paranoia already induced by the bad acid.

'At one point we had 150 kids freaked out simultaneously. I'm not talking about the kid who is a little spaced out saying, "Look baby, I don't know where I am." I mean the horrendous kind, the paranoia, muscular activity, hostility, aggression, kind of frightened-out-of-their-minds scene that is unbelievable unless you've seen it happen', Abruzzi told *LIFE*. 'The whole thing was a drag, a bust.'

Not everyone was entirely disappointed, however. No money was ever refunded to the ticket holders, no bands were paid, and someone – whose identity was never discovered – was half a million dollars better off.

3 August

2006

A young Serbian, Ratko Dankovic, had been drinking with three friends when a sword-swallowing routine came on the television. He told his friends that the act looked easy – and that anyone could do it. Naturally they challenged him, promising the princely sum of £10 if he succeeded.

One of his friends said later: 'He stood in the corner of the room and was holding this stuff above his head and swallowing it with his head tilted back, and we all thought it was just part of the act. We had no idea he was really swallowing it . . . I thought he was just pretending and then hiding it in his pockets or something.'

The astonished trio realized that something was wrong when Dankovic collapsed. They checked to see where the assorted metal items had gone – and could not find them. 'Then we realized he really had swallowed them.'

He was rushed to hospital, where an X-ray showed that he had swallowed a spoon, eight nails and an eight-inch carving knife. It took surgeons five hours to get everything out. But at least he won the bet.

4 August

1995

Ted Joffe was stopped by police at Osaka airport after the crew on his flight from Manila reported that he had refused to eat his meal, an action that led them to believe that he might have 'swallowed drugs to smuggle into Japan'. After a gruelling interrogation and internal examination Joffe was released to tell reporters, 'Next time I'll stuff the meal into the seat pocket in front of me'.

5 August

1823

Charles Green was a pioneering aeronaut. He's best remembered now for tying a horse to a hot-air balloon and taking to the skies on its back. Not all his attempts at flight were so successful, however. The most lamentable occasion has to be the day that he and his assistants failed to attach the basket properly to their balloon – a mistake they were made aware of only when the balloon began to rise and the basket stayed on the ground. This misfortune wouldn't have been half so remarkable if Mr Green hadn't then grabbed on to the balloon hoop with his colleague and made a distinctly undignified pass over Cheltenham.

6 August

1992

Today Chicago lawyer Frank D. Zafarre III filed a lawsuit against Maria Dillon for $40,310.48 in lost courting expenses.

Dillon, a 21-year-old waitress at an Italian restaurant in Chicago, had promised to marry the 44-year-old lawyer but later changed her mind, prompting him to plot revenge using an arcane piece of state law relating to broken trysts.

The figure was provisional – intended to cover the cost of a fur coat, a car, a typewriter and an engagement ring – and Zafarre said it would probably rise once he had factored in interest and a final credit card bill. Although he had been forced to go to law, Zafarre was not without hope that he and Dillon could patch things up. In a letter dated 3 August, just before he filed his lawsuit, he romantically stated that 'I am still willing to marry you on the conditions hereinbelow set forth'.

The conditions included a pledge of faith, a promise never to lie to him again 'about anything' and the enactment of the marriage ceremony within forty-five days. 'Please feel free to call me if you have any questions or would like to discuss any of the matters addressed herein', finished the honey-tongued Zafarre.

In spite of this skilful wooing, Ms Dillon told the *New York Times* that there was no chance of reconciliation. 'It makes me want to swim across Lake Michigan to the other side to get as far away as possible from him', she said. 'I can't imagine telling my children as a bedtime story that mommy and daddy got married because of a lawsuit.'

She hired a lawyer of her own, and the case was dismissed in November.

7 August

1928

Workers dredging the Chesterfield Canal discovered that the Victorian engineering marvel had a plug – when they accidentally pulled it out and watched in amazement as millions of gallons of water drained away into the nearby River Idle.

8 August

1984

Joseph Nickerson was adamant that the true sportsman respects his prey. In his partridge-obsessed autobiography *A Shooting Man's Creed* he even declared that shooting was something of a 'religion' to him. The sport, he said, required ritual, immense discipline and most of all 'love'. The prey, meanwhile – the 'splendid quarry' – were to be treated with reverence.

Strangely, however, he neglects to mention the day he himself became the 'splendid quarry' and was shot in the arse by the Deputy Prime Minister of Great Britain. The accident occurred when Willie Whitelaw (shortly to become Viscount Whitelaw) slipped in the hunting butts – and shot Nickerson in his, er, butt. Whitelaw also took down the shooting party's loader, Lindsay Waddell, who spent two days in hospital as a consequence and incidentally scored a first for British politics. Such a display of clumsy and dangerous buffoonery remained unattained by our American cousins until US Vice-President Dick Cheney shot his friend Harry Whittington in 2006 (*see* 11 February).

9 August

1994

A man in Staffanstorp, Sweden, opened his toilet to be greeted by the unusual and alarming sight of a live boa constrictor's upper regions. Naturally he panicked, and soon a huge hunt was on for the pet, which had escaped into the local sewage system when its owner had left it in a bath so it could cool off during a heatwave. The snake was eventually flushed out, but rumours persisted for years that it had been pregnant and had given birth to more killer reptiles while in the pipes.

10 August

1995

Spectators at a tennis match at Craiglockhart tennis centre in Edinburgh, Scotland, were surprised when a shower of human excrement landed on them. 'I was sitting on the ground when I heard a loud slap', said witness John Paterson. 'I looked around, and my wife's back and arms were covered.' Dozens more spectators were liberally doused with poo too, and not surprisingly, as Paterson commented, 'the smell was unbearable'.

Perplexingly, although the shit undeniably hit the fans, no one could say where it came from. Edinburgh District Council confirmed that the faeces were human, but having ruled out the aircraft that were passing overhead at the time after checking their sewage tanks, they had no further leads to follow. The origins of the brown shower remain a mystery to this day.

11 August

1984

'My fellow Americans, I'm pleased to tell you today that I've signed legislation that will outlaw Russia for ever. We begin bombing in five minutes.' Ronald Reagan's pre-radio broadcast joke quickly soured when the President discovered that his microphone was on, and that the world – including Russia – could hear him.

12 August

1822

The British politician Robert Stewart, Lord Castlereagh, one of the chief architects of the war against Napoleon, committed suicide. Inspired by Castlereagh's notorious repressive tendencies and frequently bloody attacks on political liberals, Byron wrote the following charming verse to mark the occasion:

> Posterity will ne'er survey
> A nobler grave than this.
> Here lie the bones of Castlereagh,
> Stop, traveller, and piss.

13 August

1998

Unfortunately for John Issa, his court-ordered urine test came back positive. For pregnancy. 'It was obviously not his urine', said perceptive prosecutor Werner Berthol.

Issa had been obliged to provide a sample for probation officers before being sentenced for stealing Christmas presents from doorsteps in Ohio. Suspicions had been aroused when he handed over an unusually cool sample and confirmed when it came back showing he was with child . . . not least because his wife, who accompanied him to the testing, was clearly expecting.

Issa was made to give another sample, under more stringent conditions. It tested positive for cocaine, and he was sentenced to a year in jail. 'I'm sure the judge took the tests into consideration', Barthol said.

1946

'Go away, I'm all right!' H.G. Wells ordered the doctor leaning over his death-bed. Sadly he was wrong and died minutes later.

14 August

1978

Back in the days of three-channel broadcasting it was nearly impossible for a television programme to receive zero viewing figures, but that's just what seems to have happened in France on this day, when a national network showed an in-depth interview with an Armenian woman on her fortieth birthday. A poll revealed that 67 per cent of viewers had chosen to watch a Napoleonic costume drama, and 33 per cent had opted for perennial French favourite *It's a Knock-out*. Precisely no one had chosen to engage with the Armenian's story of her marriage and illnesses, even though the newspaper *France Soir* had selected it as their choice for the evening's best viewing.

15 August

440

There was an ancient Jewish prophecy based on calculations made from the Talmud that the Messiah would arrive in the year 440. It seemed as though these predictions had come true – on the island of Crete at least – when a man calling himself Moses came forward and said he had been sent from Heaven to lead his followers back to the Promised Land. Soon, he said, he was going to make the sea part and lead his people through it, just like his ancient namesake.

When the appointed day came, hundreds followed Moses to a precipice overhanging the sea. He raised his arms, ordered the sea to separate and commanded his followers to fling themselves into the waves. Unfortunately, although dozens of followers obeyed him, the sea didn't. Those who jumped into the waters were dashed against the rocks and drowned. Moses probably perished along with them. At any rate, he was never heard of again.

16 August

1977

Elvis Presley, the king of rock and roll, died on the throne. One of the greatest entertainers in history was found on this night, aged just forty-two, in his bathroom, trousers around his ankles, hamburger in his hand (according to legend at least), struck down by heart failure.

17 August

1992

Today the Wing Wah Chinese restaurant in South Dennis, Massachusetts, was closed down for a number of health and safety violations.

'I've seen everything now', said local health director Ted Dumas, after explaining that the restaurant drained water from cabbage by putting the wet vegetable into laundry bags, placing those between two pieces of plywood and then squeezing them out by driving over them in a van.

18 August

2002

During the course of one afternoon Tyrone Hogan had already racked up a considerable tally of misdemeanours. His spree had included a kidnapping, a mugging and a car-jacking when he decided to make off with just one more van, a little beige number that was parked at a petrol station on Santa Monica Boulevard in Los Angeles.

His one-man crime wave was brought to an abrupt halt, however, shortly after he entered the vehicle and discovered that packed into the back were the irate members of a local judo club. Within seconds Hogan was out on the floor of the garage forecourt, underneath a number of skilled martial artists. 'We had this guy like a pretzel on the ground', said Nestor Bustillo, the club's judo instructor.

'He was detained, to say the least', said the policeman who came to pick him up. 'Judo team 1, car-jacker 0.'

19 August

1993

Things had been going well for practising Satanist Alvin Lastimado Jr. He'd kidnapped a girl, and all he had to do now was chant out a special incantation and . . . damn it. He realized that he couldn't remember all the words of the liturgy he'd been trying to memorize. So he dashed out of his house to the local library to refresh his memory. While he was there, the woman escaped and called the police. They arrested Lastimado in the occult section.

20 August

1992

The curious expression 'toe-job' entered the English language when UK paper the *Daily Mirror* published pictures of Texan businessman John Bryan sucking on the feet of Sarah Ferguson, the Duchess of York, as she reclined topless by a swimming pool. Mr Bryan, who had hitherto officially been described as the business adviser to the estranged wife of Prince Andrew, initially attempted to persuade the Press Complaints Commission to prevent publication of the photos. When that failed, he changed tack and eventually sold the press a kiss-and-tell story of his adventures with British royalty for £250,000.

Another interesting expression gained popular currency thanks to this event when, combined with a rather nasty fire in Windsor Castle and the separation of Prince Charles and Princess Diana, it caused the Queen to describe 1992 as an *annus horribilis*.

21 August

2006

The Chinese state media reported that a Mrs Li today gave in to what she saw as her dog's frequent requests to drive her car. She had noticed how keen the animal was on crouching behind the wheel and thought it would be only kind to let it try to control the vehicle for itself. While she operated the accelerator and the brake, she left the dog to do the steering. Almost immediately the pair crashed into an oncoming truck. They emerged uninjured, but with tails firmly between their legs.

22 August

1995

The first wild otter to be seen in the UK for almost forty years was discovered – when a naturalist in Nottinghamshire accidentally ran it over with his car.

23 August

2006

After a night of drinking Richard Gonzales made a valiant attempt to get back to his home in Arkansas. He nearly made it too. He fell only at the very last hurdle, when he passed out unconscious in his own driveway. Fortunately, shortly after midnight his wife returned home to wake him. Unfortunately, she woke him by running him over in her car, having failed to spot his prone body in front of her. Miraculously he escaped with only minor cuts and scratches.

24 August

1982

On this afternoon in 1982 thirty-year-old Harry Seigler was on trial for murder. He'd been accused of slashing the throat of insurance agent Douglas Mitchell and, because he was in Virginia, faced death by electrocution if found guilty.

It was 6.30 p.m. The jury had been out deliberating their verdict for three and a half hours, and his defence team were getting correspondingly worried. They decided to gamble, entering into a plea-bargain agreement with the prosecuting counsel, Warren Von Such. It was agreed that if Seigler pleaded guilty to a lesser charge, he would receive a sixty-year sentence instead of the electric chair.

After Seigler pleaded guilty, he was led away and the judge invited the jury back into the room to tell them what had happened. One slumped in his chair, another bolted straight upright. Several others just moaned. The reason for their distress? They'd just found Seigler not guilty.

It was too late. Having pleaded guilty, Seigler had to serve his sentence. He wasn't even going to be eligible for parole for twelve years. 'I can't tell you how badly he feels', said one of his defence lawyers. Meanwhile, when Prosecutor Von Such was apprised of the facts, he summed up the situation most succinctly. 'Holy mackerel!' he said.

25 August

1835

'Celestial discoveries!' proclaimed today's *New York Sun*. 'We have just learned from an eminent publisher in this city that Sir John Herschel at the Cape of Good Hope has made some astronomical discoveries of the most wonderful description, by means of an immense telescope of an entirely new principle.'

The paper's young reporter, Richard Locke (a direct descendant of the famous philosopher John Locke), seemed to have one of the scoops of the century. His subsequent description of the mechanics of Sir John's astonishing new telescope and its ability to make out minute details on the moon was soon the hottest news in town.

As the paper's circulation grew, Locke fed his hungry public more and more fascinating details. A few days after the first article he revealed that Herschel had made out strange animals wandering around on the moon: 'lunar quadrupeds', giant lumbering beasts with 'fleshy appendages' over their eyes.

On 28 August came the news that there were human-like creatures (with wings!) visible on the lunar surface, and the world was enraptured. 'We scientifically denominated them the vespertilio-homo – or manbat', wrote Locke.

Circulation leapt to 19,360, making the *Sun*, as it proudly proclaimed, the best-selling paper in the world. Meanwhile the story was translated into French and circulated from London to Delhi. The *New York Times* became caught up in the frenzy too. The report was, opined the US paper of record, 'probable and plausible'.

On 31 August, however, there was bad news. The telescope had broken, and there would be no further reports from the moon for quite some time. The truth was that, having attained huge circulation for his paper, Locke had decided it was time to kill the story. A few days later he revealed the deception to another journalist in a drunken conversation, and soon the worldwide media were reporting that they had known that Locke's story was a pack of lies from the start.

Owing to the slowness of travel to South Africa in those days, Sir John Herschel didn't discover that he had taken part in the century's biggest hoax for several months. Posterity has not recorded his reaction when he was eventually told.

26 August

2002

Jean Curtis filed for divorce after catching her husband making love to another bird: a frozen chicken. The 47-year-old from Manchester explained to the *Sun* newspaper that she found him in their front room dressed in her silk blouse and stockings and with the frozen poultry in a most inappropriate place. 'My jaw just dropped', Ms Curtis told a reporter from the tabloid. 'I said, "You dirty bastard, that's my Sunday lunch".'

27 August

1999

Seventeen-year-old Lucas Winter's attempt to rob a bank in Oregon went seriously wrong when he managed to lock himself in the boot of his own getaway car. Investigators later surmised that his idea had been to rob the bank, make a quick change in his car and drive away to safety. The first part of his plan went relatively smoothly. He walked into a bank wearing a distinctive red shirt and white hat, grabbed a handful of cash and ran for the street.

Next, he had intended to grab a change of clothes and quit the scene of the crime. However, nothing more was heard from him until forty minutes later, when policeman Daryl Johnson was walking through a car park a couple of blocks from the recently robbed bank and heard a thumping noise coming from the back of a car and someone pleading to be let out.

'He was probably hoping that it was someone other than a police officer', said Roberts, who rescued the hot and understandably distraught Winters – and then arrested him.

28 August

2006

Martin Nolan paid £200 and spent seven hours in severe pain in order to get a prayer tattooed on his back in tribute to his mum. When he got home he discovered that, with cruel irony, the word 'wisdom' in the prayer had been misspelled as 'nisdom'.

1948

Margaret Allen, a 42-year-old bus conductress from Rawenstall, Lancashire, killed Nancy Chadwick, a 68-year-old lady who used to tell fortunes in a local park, with a hammer. 'I was in one of my funny moods', Allen later explained.

29 August

2001

It was a dark, wet night, and a speeding Honda was skidding all over the rain-slicked road in Largo, Florida, much to the alarm of police officer George Edmiston, who set off in hot pursuit. In spite of the difficult conditions, Roel Pena Sevilla, the driver of the Honda, managed to execute a tight right turn off the highway when he saw the patrol car chasing him. 'I think he was trying to lose me', said Edmiston later.

It would have worked too, but for one thing: Sevilla had turned off into the car park of the Largo Police Department. He was arrested shortly afterwards, and his bad day got worse when the victim of the hit-and-run he'd been speeding away from turned up to file a complaint and spotted his car, still steaming, in the car park.

30 August

1997

Detective-Sergeant Daniel Edwards was found crushed between his patrol car and a tree near Cape Town, South Africa. Coroners said it appeared the policeman had parked his car on an embankment before stepping out to relieve himself against the tree. The car had rolled down the slope and killed him.

31 August

2006

David Miliband was the first British government minister to start communicating his thoughts on an internet blog and renowned as one of the most techno-savvy members of the New Labour spin machine. Today he attempted to enhance his pioneering reputation by putting up a draft version of a government document on the internet and inviting comments and contributions from members of the public.

The document was described as an 'environmental contract' setting out the responsibilities of the government and the public in trying to protect the earth's delicate eco-system. The interesting thing about it was that it included a system similar to that used on the Wikipedia website to allow the public to change the wording and include their own contributions. They didn't need to be asked twice.

Within just a couple of hours hundreds of internerds had visited Miliband's page and given it a complete overhaul. What was once a rather jargon-heavy piece of propaganda now began with the following delightful introduction:

> Hi there. I'm David, Dave, Miliband. I've set up this big conversation in cyberspace here to try and create a news story

based around the fact that New Labour (and me especially) really want to know what the public think about the environment . . . Also, look at my beautiful face.

Practical suggestions from the public on environmental stewardship included the idea that 'the likes of Jeremy Clarkson, in promoting pollution, should be penalized thrice over' and that taxpayers 'pay a higher proportion of their income to the government, and see little tangible improvement in their standard of living'.

Meanwhile, 'spade, organic yoghurt stirrer, old washing-up liquid bottle [and] sticky back plastic' were suggested as the tools that 'can be used to deliver the environmental contract'. A list of items that 'create the right incentive frameworks' was changed so that it included 'big stick' and (oddly) 'owl magnet'.

Finally the wording was changed so that the minister made the following frank confession: 'We just can't help but meddle, interfere, impose our views on others, and generally use taxpayers' resources in ways that are wasteful except in our own self-aggrandisement.'

Not surprisingly, the 'Wiki' function was quickly taken off the page, and the experiment abandoned.

September

1 September

2002

Sixty-three-year-old Giovanni Greco's obsession with the grave proved to be particularly unhealthy on this day in 2002. He was fond of making regular weekend visits to his mausoleum as workers constructed it in his hometown of Lascari, but this one was cut short when he slipped on a ladder leading to the top of the structure, hit his head on a marble step and fell dead into his own tomb.

2 September

1666

At 3 a.m. the Lord Mayor of London was annoyed to be woken by news of a fire in Pudding Lane in London. He dutifully went to investigate but was signally unimpressed. 'Pish! A woman might piss it out', he exclaimed before returning to bed. Of course, his assessment was proved completely wrong. The fire went on burning uncontrollably until 6 September, destroying more than 13,000 houses, 87 churches, 4 bridges, 44 company halls and numerous prisons.

3 September

1752

This date caused considerable alarm when it did not occur. The UK and US colonies caught up with the date in the rest of Europe by swapping from the old-fashioned Julian calendar to the Gregorian one, and Wednesday 2 September was followed by Thursday 14 September. The change proved traumatic. Legend has it that there were widespread riots as the populace demanded back the eleven days that they had lost, and equally widespread attacks on landlords who were accused of manufacturing the date-shift so that they could charge an extra week-and-a-half's rent at the end of the shortened month.

4 September

1994

Brazilian finance minister Ruben Ricupero thought he was speaking off the record when he cheerfully informed TV reporters that he frequently lied about the health of the economy to make his government look good and boasted that his party used government resources to boost their own presidential candidate. Not only was he on the record, however, but his words were broadcast live to an astonished nation.

Ricupero was in a break between taping two television interviews for the national Globo television network and thought he could relax and amuse reporters, but, unbeknown to him, technicians failed to stop the tapes rolling.

'Listen, just between us, it might seem presumptuous, but the government needs me a lot more than I need it', Mr. Ricupero began, little realizing that viewers all over the country could hear him. 'I have no scruples', he announced proudly, when the conversation moved on to economic indicators. 'What is good, we take advantage of. What is bad, we hide.'

Asked why his government had lowered petrol prices the week before, he said brightly, 'Every once in a while, you have to create confusion. There is no doubt about it – this isn't a rational country.'

After fifteen minutes of such enjoyable banter a technician informed the men that there had been a slip-up and they were still on air. 'So they got it?' Ricupero asked, suddenly only too aware that this cosy TV studio talk could well be his last.

'Yes.'

The next day he appeared at a press conference, tears in his eyes, proclaiming that he was the 'victim of an electronic breakdown' and that his remarks had been taken 'out of context'. Then he resigned.

5 September

2002

At 10 a.m. on this Thursday morning a New York office worker, Tripp Murray, sent a chatty e-mail to Mary Callahan, a woman he'd recently taken on a date, suggesting that they might get together again.

He was surprised to receive a reply entitled 'All Time Low' and starting, 'OK, first — here is the e-mail I received from Tripp, the new guy I met last week'. Then he was no doubt horrified as he went on to read Callahan explaining how easy this 'Tripp' would be to drain of money: 'Since we have not slept together, he will of course be trying to impress me and will, therefore, do anything I ask.'

Callahan had hit the 'Reply' button instead of 'Forward', an embarrassment that can only have been compounded by the fact that she went on to detail how a recent partner had fallen asleep on her during sex.

Tripp promptly forwarded the message on to a co-worker, James Salter. Salter forwarded it to several others, with the message: 'Drop what you're doing and read this. The following is an exchange between a friend of a guy that sits on our desk and a girl he took out on a date. Read from the bottom up. Oh my Lord.'

'Ugly dating scene in NYC', observed one recipient, Sam Greene, before hitting 'Send'. 'Sucks to be that girl this morning!'

Soon the e-mail reached critical mass. 'How fast until it hits the entire eastern seaboard?' one sender asked on the afternoon of Friday the 6th, as he continued to forward it on. The e-mail 'seemed to have made its way around Wall Street', wrote another. On Monday morning it was still going. 'These things spread fast, thought I'd help out', one wrote.

By 11 September the e-mail had reached Britain and Spain. By 12 September it was in Australia, now containing the instruction: 'Like the rest of the world, go straight to the bottom and read up'.

6 September

1978

A crew member accidentally dropped a paint-scraper into the torpedo hold of the US nuclear submarine *Swordfish*. The paint-scraper was at the time valued at 60 cents. The subsequent repairs cost $171,000 and put the submarine out of action for weeks while it was dry-docked.

7 September

2002

A pet hamster caused chaos in the northern English holiday town of Cleveleys, near Blackpool, when it tore down a pavement in a mini racing-car. The hamster, which quickly earned the nickname 'Speedy', was powering the car with a treadmill-style running wheel. He was, according to witnesses, running 'furiously'. His erratic journey was eventually halted when the police were called and they came and quite literally picked him up.

'This is', said PC Quentin Allen, 'the most unusual case I have ever come across.'

8 September

1986

According to the results of a 1987 libel trial against the *Daily Star*, this is one of the nights that UK Tory politician and best-selling author Jeffrey Archer did not spend with the prostitute Monica Coghlan. He was able to produce alibis for both of the occasions that the paper suggested he might have been misbehaving – 8 and 9 September – while the £2,000 he was photographed giving to Coghlan in a brown envelope was explained as the action of a philanthropist rather than, as she suggested, payment for sexual favours.

As if all that wasn't funny enough, the summing-up by the judge has gone down as one of the most barking mad in the British justice system's long and ignoble history. 'Remember Mary Archer in the witness-box', he instructed the jury. 'Your vision of her probably will never disappear. Has she elegance? Has she fragrance? Would she have, without the strain of this trial, radiance? How would she appeal? Has she had a happy married life? Has she been able to enjoy, rather than endure, her husband Jeffrey?' The judge then went on to say of Jeffrey Archer, alarmingly: 'Is he in need of cold, unloving, rubber-insulated sex in a seedy hotel round about quarter to one on a Tuesday morning after an evening at the Caprice?'

'No' was clearly the conclusion he had made, and Archer emerged from the whole affair smelling almost as fragrant as his wife. He won £500,000 damages, which he claimed he was going to donate to charity – although no record of what happened to the money seems to exist.

The scales of justice finally started to tip back against Archer in 1999, when his friend Ted Francis admitted that he had fabricated an alibi for the peer on 9 September 1987. Ironically, as the subsequent perjury trial proved, that wasn't even the night when Archer had his assignation with Coghlan. His secretary had been keeping detailed records of his movements all along and showed that he'd actually been with Coghlan on the 8th. Archer, whom the then Tory leader William Hague had recently described as the candidate of 'probity and integrity' in the London mayoral elections, went to jail.

9 September

1999

On 9/9/99 all sorts of cosmologists and numerologists were getting excited. Nostradamus had predicted a meteor strike on earth around then, and the fact that the number was used as a termination code in many computer programmes just *had* to mean something.

No one was getting more wound up than the members of a small cult in the village of Sukmajaya, Indonesia, however. Because they believed that the world was going to end, cult members had sold all their worldly possessions. Nine days before the big event members had also locked themselves in their houses. This latter enforced imprisonment may explain why they lost control so dramatically when the world failed to end and beat three of their own members to death. 'The members were really mad', explained Saadi Arsam, village chief.

10 September

1087

William the Conqueror died in France. The death itself was said to be swift and unremarkable, but the aftermath was gruesome. William, a notorious glutton, was too fat for any coffin, and during his funeral it was discovered that his body was too large for the masonry grave created for him. The burial party proceeded to force the victor of the Battle of Hastings into the hole, whereupon the gases that had been gathering in the old king's gut exploded and the body burst. The resultant stench drove those attending the funeral out of the church 'in horror and disgust', according to the nineteenth-century writer Robert Chambers, who also added gnomically: 'Such was the end of one of the greatest potentates who ever lived – one who had driven human beings before him like cattle, but never induced any one to love him, not even one of his own children.'

11 September

2006

Religious zealot David Robert McMenemy had been wandering the Midwest of the USA since August, looking for an abortion clinic to attack in order to make a memorable protest against women's right to choose. Today he finally found a target and drove his car through the door of the Edgerton Women's Health Center in Davenport, Iowa. His car came to rest in the middle of the room but didn't catch fire as he'd hoped. Unperturbed, McMenemy pulled out a Gatorade bottle full of petrol that he'd already prepared, poured it over the car and set it on fire. Unfortunately for McMenemy, but luckily for everyone else, the building's sprinkler system put out the fire, and no one was hurt as the Christian had intended. Even more upsetting from McMenemy's point of view, however, was the revelation that the building was not an abortion centre at all. It was just a general female health clinic and didn't even refer women for abortions.

'Our commander on the scene was very surprised, by the whole thing', said a fireman afterwards.

12 September

1921

Calvin Coolidge is renowned as one of the most taciturn Presidents in US history. One of his favourite tricks was to sit silently through interviews, explaining that he did so because 'Many times I say only "yes" or "no" to people. Even that is too much. It winds them up for twenty minutes more.'

One of the most onerous burdens that fell on this silent man was the necessity to attend numerous parties when he was Vice-President, then largely a social appointment. According to legend, he was at one of these functions on this date when he trumped the famous wit Dorothy Parker. She turned to him early on in the evening and informed him that she had made a bet that she would be able to get 'more than two words' out of him. 'You lose', replied Coolidge, who sat in silence for the rest of the meal.

Parker got her revenge when Coolidge's death was announced twelve years later. 'How can they tell?' she asked.

13 September

1990

Twenty-five-year-old Ottawa resident Danny Simpson was today given six years in jail for stealing £6,000 from a bank using an elderly Colt .45 pistol. His misery at being caught wasn't at all assuaged by the knowledge that, when his gun was impounded by police, it was recognized as a collectors' item. It emerged that the weapon was a fine example of a rare First World War production of the famous Colt line made under licence by the Ross Rifle Company in Quebec City. At the time of Simpson's arrest it was said to be worth at least £12,000 and possibly as much as £100,000.

In other words, if Simpson had just walked into a shop and legally sold the gun, he would have made twice as much as from his failed robbery attempt. And while he mouldered away in jail, the gun was given pride of place in a Canadian museum.

14 September

2006

When 35-year-old Zoran Nikolovic approached a witch doctor with a rather delicate problem, he was promised total discretion and 100 per cent success. Instead, he became a media star with a ruined manhood.

Zoran was worried that he was ejaculating prematurely when having sex. The witch doctor told him the best way to cure it was to sodomize a hedgehog. Foolishly, Zoran believed him – and checked into hospital soon afterwards with severe lacerations.

A spokesperson for the hospital later told the amused reporters of the world's press that fortunately the hedgehog was unharmed and that the luckless Nikolovic had come off far worse from the encounter. 'No one here has ever come across anything like it', he said. 'And I doubt any of us ever will again.'

15 September

1896

In 1896 the beautifully named William Crush, a passenger agent for the Missouri, Kansas and Texas railroad, hit on a brilliant idea.

He'd noticed that, whenever there was a train crash, hundreds of people would come from miles around to gawp at the wreckage and mangled victims. If, he thought, people knew beforehand when a crash would occur and facilities were set up for them to view it properly, thousands might be attracted.

He was proved abundantly correct. Following a media blitz, 50,000 people turned out on the morning of 15 September to the special siding he had persuaded his railway company to build for the event. There was a tent village, a grandstand and a bandstand. There were restaurants, lemonade stalls and games booths.

The crowds were given the whole day to spend their money. 'A wonderful wrecklessness marked the conduct of many', wrote one punning reporter. Then, at 5 p.m. two old locomotives which had been refurbished and painted red and green for the purpose slowly shunted up to each other and kissed noses. After that they backed up until they were a mile apart, and William Crush dropped a white flag. The engine drivers threw the throttles open and jumped clear as the two trains powered towards each other, the roar of the crowd barely audible above the pounding pistons and screaming whistles.

On impact the trains are said to have reared up against each other like fighting stallions, before collapsing back down to the ground with earth-shaking force. The crowd went wild. Their delight was soon turned to terror, however, when the two engines' boilers exploded simultaneously (an outcome that, somehow, nobody had foreseen). Twisted metal and shrapnel rained down, killing two and injuring countless others as the gathered horde fled for their lives. A cow, quietly grazing half a mile away, was crushed by a flying smokestack.

The next day William Crush was fired.

16 September

2006

'Described as a true public servant who takes pleasure giving back to the community, Chris Sharek is the new face of civil engineering who really shines in the sunshine state.' That's what it said on Chris Sharek's calling card, but his bright image was muddied when he took his father-in-law for a drive in the wilderness near his home in Venice, Florida, and got his four-wheel-drive stuck in several feet of the brown stuff.

When the local authorities turned up, they were faced with a scene of dirty devastation. The crime report from the officer on the scene is a master class in inadvertent slapstick comedy:

> After off-roading (mudding) inside the park all afternoon, the men got both their vehicles stuck in the park. It was at this time that the men called some friends to come pull them out . . . Once the friends gained access to the park, they also got stuck. Then even more people were called . . . By the time it was all said and done, there were 2 Jeeps, 2 pick-ups, 1 Hummer, and 1 tractor in an area closed to vehicles.

In total, Sharek had managed to trap six vehicles for eleven hours and made a huge mess of an area of prime wilderness that no car was supposed to enter.

When asked if he knew what he was doing was against the law, he responded 'I suppose'. He later qualified this by admitting 'it was a bad decision'. This 'shining public servant' no doubt felt especially sheepish because of his job. He was the area utilities director and therefore in charge of ensuring that the city complied with environmental laws.

17 September

1932

Struggling actress Peg Entwistle, despairing of ever getting a decent role to play, made her way to the famous Hollywood sign in Los Angeles, climbed the maintenance ladder to the top of the giant H and jumped. Her body was found the next morning, and she was pronounced dead. Two days later, in one of those bitter twists that makes you wonder at the sardonic sense of humour of the universe, her uncle opened a letter to her offering her the lead role in a stage production. According to legend, her character was supposed to commit suicide in the final act.

18 September

1984

Today the residents of Antelope in Oregon received a nasty surprise. They realized that their quiet and hitherto conservative town had been renamed Rajneeshpuram.

The change had been effected by the disciples of Bhagwan Shree Rajneesh. Such huge numbers of the orange-robed followers of this Indian guru had moved on to a ranch just outside Antelope that they far outnumbered the original residents and were able to win any vote on the local council . . . and so it was that they renamed the town and signalled the start of a long and crazy battle.

Locals were soon afterwards alarmed to realize that men with Uzi machine guns were patrolling the grounds of the ranch – and that its borders had been marked off with barbed-wire fences and watchtowers. Meanwhile it emerged that Bhagwan Shree Rajneesh himself had taken a vow of silence and that his disciples were effectively led by his out-of-control henchwoman Ma Anand Sheela.

When locals started to protest at these and other dubious activities, Sheela responded by having her followers dump salmonella into the salad bars of several restaurants. Antelope therefore gained the dubious distinction of being the site of the first (and to date, the last) successful bio-terrorism attack in US history.

Eventually Bhagwan Rajneesh emerged from his silence and attempted to distance himself from his disciples. He said that Sheela had been running the place like a 'fascist concentration camp'. He also called on the FBI to conduct an independent investigation into the ranch. The FBI quickly found an extensive eavesdropping system that was wired throughout the commune residences, public buildings and offices. They also uncovered a secret laboratory where experiments had been run on the manufacture of HIV as well as salmonella. Oddest of all, they found that Rajneesh's bedroom was rigged up so that he could receive nitrous oxide – laughing gas – while he lay in bed. (Trivia fans will be interested to learn that it has been estimated he took more than any human before or since, largely through spigots that were attached to the walls wherever he lived.)

Sheela confessed to having a rather 'bad habit' of poisoning people and was sent to jail. Bhagwan Shree Rajneesh himself was charged with criminal conspiracy, thirty-four counts of making false statements to federal officials and two counts of immigration fraud. He paid a $400,000 fine and was given a ten-year sentence – suspended on the understanding that he would leave the USA. When he left, he declared that he 'hoped never to come back'.

On 6 November 1985, the remaining residents voted by 34 votes to 0 to restore Rajneeshpuram to its original name of Antelope.

19 September

1997

When out motoring, there are few things more annoying than being cut up by another driver. Even so, it's probably safe to say that when a car swerved in front of David Cline in Durham, North Carolina, he over-reacted. Especially since he was a driving instructor with two fifteen-year-old pupils in his car.

When the luckless John Macklin performed the manoeuvre that so enraged Cline, the instructor wasn't even at the wheel: one of his pupils was. So great was his ire, however, that he ordered his fifteen-year-old charge to give chase. She did, and finally caught up with Macklin at a set of traffic lights. Thereupon Cline leapt from the vehicle, started shouting abuse at his enemy and hit him full on the face through his open car window.

At this stage Cline seems to have lost the will to fight. At any rate, he charged back to his own car and ordered his young driver to speed away from the scene. The hunter became the hunted as Macklin gunned after them, intent on writing down their licence plate number.

It was then that the police became involved. They pulled over the driving instructor's vehicle for speeding, their bemusement at seeing a fifteen-year-old girl at the wheel only compounded when the bloody-faced Macklin ran up to them.

When it became clear what had happened, Cline was arrested for assault and released on a $400 bond. No action was taken against the girl driver.

20 September

1736

Samuel Baldwin's last wishes were carried out, and his dead body was thrown into the sea, not because he was a sailor but because he wanted to prevent his wife from achieving her frequently stated ambition of dancing on his grave.

21 September

2006

The Ethnic Minority Games were under way in south-western China. This feel-good event was supposed, according to their chief organizer, Ren Muzhen, to 'develop the minorities' characteristic sports, build up their health and increase national unity'.

Sadly, the atmosphere at the event wasn't quite as harmonious as the authorities hoped. There had already been some controversy after competitors complained about 'big women with Adam's apples' who were taking part in the female Dragon Boat race, and referees discovered that the suspect athletes were actually men wearing wigs. However, the real crunch came today, after the final of the wrestling competition, when the team from host city, Zhaotong, and their deadly rivals from Wenshan refused to stop fighting after the result was called. Referees and officials were powerless to stop the brawl, which only ended when the Zhaotong team called in a local gang, who chased away the Wenshan team with knives and sticks.

'I've never seen violence and ugliness like that', a reporter at the games told the Chinese news agency Xinhua sadly.

22 September

1923

The world heavyweight boxing match between Gene Tunney and Jack Dempsey was one of the strangest and most controversial of all time. The main point of contention was the extra-slow count the referee gave for Tunney after Dempsey knocked him to the canvas, which allowed him to get up, fight on and eventually take the victory. Three radio listeners are said to have died of heart attacks brought on by the tension of this delay. Meanwhile the excitement of Tunney's eventual win caused another near-fatality in a delighted fan. His frenzied waving and shouting wouldn't have been a problem if he hadn't been holding an ice-pick in his hand and stabbed himself in the head with it.

23 September

1990

Like many people, Vermont resident Edward Brisson enjoyed reading on the toilet and often took a magazine with him when he visited the lavatory. Unlike many people, however, his daily ritual was interrupted by a lorry. A truck weighing several tons today crashed through the wall of his house and dumped its load on Brisson, who was left sitting on the toilet, his trousers lowered, up to his shoulders in sand.

Observing that the truck itself had missed him by just seven or eight feet, Mr Brisson later told the press how lucky he felt. 'A little closer and he would have had me', he said, adding with considerable understatement, 'It was strange.'

24 September

2002

On this day the sheriff's department in Coldwater, Michigan, which had been researching complaints of possible telemarketing fraud in their area, passed on the following information to local news organizations:

> In the course of our investigation, it was learned that this is going on throughout the United States and some of these telemarketing programmes are believed to be operated by Al-Qaeda. The CIA has announced that they acquired a video-tape showing Al-Qaeda members making phone solicitations for vacation home rentals, long distance telephone service, magazine subscriptions and other products.

This bizarre and alarming news was repeated on several local radio stations before Dan Nichols, the detective responsible for the release, was informed that his source for the story was a joke. The article he'd been reading (headline: 'Report: Al-Qaeda Allegedly Engaging in Telemarketing') actually came from the 18 September edition of the famous spoof website The Onion. The alert was cancelled.

'It felt like I'd been had', commented the philosophical Nichols. 'I was just kind of ticked off at myself for not verifying it before I passed it along, and not making sure it was satire. I have no problem with satire. I enjoy a good joke. I just hate it when it's on me.'

25 September

2003

Calvin Miller, a prison inmate who was angry with one of his former criminal colleagues, decided to get his revenge. Miller, who appropriately enough went under the moniker 'Cheesy Rat', grassed up his erstwhile ally for his involvement in a double murder in 1995 in Kansas City. Working on the tip, police were able to figure out the exact sequence of events that led to the killing and arrested Miller's enemy together with two other men.

Unfortunately for Mr Miller, the police also worked out the identity of the gang's ringleader: Cheesy Rat himself. They also discovered that it was he who fired the shotgun that blasted the luckless victims from the face of the earth.

Cheesy Rat was sentenced to seventeen further years in jail – far longer than the man he had fingered. 'I guess I was pretty stupid', he commented with some accuracy after the sentence was passed.

26 September

1998

Preacher Melvyn Nurse wanted to show the congregation at the ironically named Livingway Christian Fellowship Church International in Jacksonville, Florida, that sin is as dangerous as Russian roulette. To dramatize his point he'd brought along a Magnum .357 loaded with one blank cartridge. His intention was to go through each of the seven deadly sins, spin the gun's chamber and hold the gun to his head.

A vivid demonstration of just how risky it can be to play Russian roulette was given when Nurse reached the second sin, fired the gun and the cardboard wad from the blank cartridge shot into his temple.

'I thought it was part of the sermon, that he was supposed to fall', said Anthony Speight, the church pastor. He realized that this might not be the case when he saw blood on the carpet. Nurse, who had apparently been unaware of the dangers of blank cartridges, was rushed to hospital, where he died several days later.

27 September

2005

Newspapers in the UK were today astonished to report that a hospital in Halifax had banned cooing at babies. On the wards staff were handing out little postcards featuring a cartoon of an unusually eloquent baby stating, 'I am small and precious so treat me with privacy and respect . . . My parents ask you to treat my personal space with consideration.' In one area there was even a doll featuring the message 'What makes you think I want to be looked at?'

'Cooing should be a thing of the past because these are little people with the same rights as you or me', explained Debbie Lawson, a manager at the Calderdale Royal Hospital's neo-natal unit, presumably thinking that that would set the record straight.

28 September

2006

'Muthuvatti Abdul is lucky to be alive', a spokesman for the Salmaniya Medical Complex told reporters in Bahrain. 'The damage is not irreparable and we are confident we can fix him. He is active, and able to digest normal food, and in a few days from now we will perform further surgery on his large intestine; but in my thirty years as a surgeon, I have never before seen such a case. Let this be a warning to all workers not to play jokes on each other with high-pressure air hoses.'

Speaking from his hospital bed, Mr Abdul himself later clarified this somewhat bewildering message with a succinct and painful explanation of the day's earlier events.

'I had been sandblasting with my friend Shams, and we were covered in sand. So we stripped off naked and turned the hoses on ourselves, to clean ourselves', he said. 'I was bending over when Shams inserted the nozzle up my rectum and gave me a quick blast of air. He only did it for a few seconds. It was a joke, that's all. But I asked him to do it again out of interest. When he did, I immediately felt myself blowing up. I knew something inside was clearly wrong. So I came here to the hospital, where they examined me, and told me that the rush of air had burst my large intestine, and created an opening in my bowel. I have telephoned my family back in India to tell them I am off work, but they do not yet know why. They will be shocked when they hear the full story.'

29 September

2000

US President George W. Bush had more good news for the world. 'I know the human being and fish can co-exist peacefully', he told a conference.

1938

On this day in 1938 British Prime Minister Neville Chamberlain, French Prime Minister Edouard Daladier and the German and

Italian dictators Adolf Hitler and Benito Mussolini signed the Munich agreement, giving over most of Czechoslovakia to Nazi Germany on the condition that Hitler expanded no further.

When Neville Chamberlain returned he told reporters in the UK, 'My good friends, for the second time in our history, a British Prime Minister has returned from Germany bringing peace with honour. I believe it is peace for our time.'

Meanwhile, Alexis Leger, a French aide, said the agreement was a relief. 'Yes, a relief. Like crapping in your pants.'

30 September

2006

Steve Wynn, a casino mogul and deep-pocketed art collector, started this evening in a very good mood. Not surprising really, considering that he'd just closed a deal to sell one of his paintings, *La Rêve*, by Pablo Picasso, for a whopping $139 million – at that time the most that had ever been paid for a picture.

So pleased was he that he invited a few guests up to his private offices to have a look at the valuable masterpiece. Among the guests was Nora Ephron, a screenwriter and blogger on the popular *Huffington Post* website. She later wrote that Wynn explained all about the origins of the painting and the intriguing fact that the face of the subject (who was one of Picasso's mistresses) is split in two – and one of the halves looks like a penis. Then she says that Wynn, who was well known for his expansive hand gestures, and who also suffers from retinitis pigmentosa, an eye disease affecting peripheral vision, raised his hand to demonstrate something about the painting and crashed his elbow right through the canvas. There was 'a terrible noise', and Wynn stepped forward to reveal there was a hole in the $139 million painting.

'Oh shit', said Wynn. 'Look what I've done.' Then he added, with considerable nobility: 'Thank God it was me.'

The biggest deal in art history was called off, and Wynn sent the painting to be repaired.

1955

The actor James Dean died in a head-on car crash. 'My fun days are over', he stated accurately just before breathing his last.

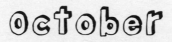

October

1 October

2006

An officer called to a domestic dispute in Auckland, New Zealand, found an argument between a couple and their teenage son raging. He attempted to reason with them but, fearing violence, resorted to using his newly issued Taser gun. His aim was to stun and subdue the father, but his first shot missed him and hit the family cat. The animal died. His second shot also missed the father but did make successful contact with his son, who fell to the ground. By that time the officer had to remove the spent cartridges from his weapon. When he did so, however, he forgot to wait for the Taser's discharge cycle to complete. Which is why he himself received a 50,000-volt blast.

When he had recovered, he tried two more shots, but these both hit the ceiling. Sensibly, he then abandoned the Taser and opted for old-fashioned pepper spray. Sadly, this too missed its intended target, and the hapless constable unloaded the noxious gas right into the face of the family's teenaged daughter, who had just that wrong moment entered the room.

At this point, no doubt fearing for the further well-being of his family and property, the father gave himself up and allowed the officer to arrest him.

2 October

2002

US investment firm Bear Stearns fell victim to a clerical error on this day in 2002. They ordered a sale of $4 billion worth of stock instead of $4 million. A spokesman for the company was upbeat about the problem, saying the company only lost 152 times what they had intended . . .

Their embarrassment was compounded the very next day, when the *Wall Street Journal* carried news of this little mistake right next to a large advert for Bear Stearns proclaiming their ability to 'execute complex transactions flawlessly'. The story was moved to a less embarrassing part of the paper in later editions.

3 October

1998

A 56-year-old father of four from Seaford, Victoria, Australia, today lost the election he was standing in against the current Prime Minister, John Howard, and found himself in the middle of a five-year battle to keep the name he had recently taken for himself: Prime Minister John Piss the Family Court and Legal Aid.

Prime Minister John Piss the Family Court and Legal Aid (or John Piss for short) had taken on his new name when he stood in protest against child support policy in Australia. When he lost the election, and the Registrar of Births, Marriages and Deaths then refused him permission to change his name legally, he took them to court.

'Mr Piss the Family Court and Legal Aid has been entered on the electoral role, and has Telstra, taxation and banking records all sent to him', his lawyer told the initial tribunal, claiming that the Registrar was discriminating against his client. 'It is important not to extract the piss and treat it as an obscenity, but [to view the word] in its meaning as to discharge or get rid of', he said.

In spite of this impressive argumentation, the case was lost, and life became even more frustrating for John when his attempts to go international with his new moniker also ran into trouble: the passport office withdrew his passport. 'If it is offensive, it's contended that doesn't make the slightest difference', said his lawyer when launching a new legal action. 'It's simply a name, full stop.'

The defence, however, drew the court's attention to 'piss' in both the *Shorter Oxford English Dictionary* and the *Macquarie Dictionary*, and the case was closed, much to the disappointment of John Piss, who was left looking for a new name. His lawyer was upset too. He had considerable stock invested in winning the case. Not least because he'd changed his own name to Abolish Child Support and Family Court.

1533

At 8.01 a.m. Michael Stifel's prediction that the world would end at 8.00 a.m. was proved erroneous. The citizens of the town of Lochau, who up until that point had been unsure whether to believe him, rewarded him with a severe flogging.

4 October

2006

David Clutterbuck, a 72-year-old Conservative councillor, today found himself the laughing-stock of the nation thanks to a joke he had recently forwarded on to fellow council members at Bournemouth Borough Council.

Ironically enough, the joke itself was decidedly unfunny: a description of the trouble Noah would have floating his ark nowadays, thanks to the need to consult planning rules, building regulations, environmental impact studies, fire and safety regulations and the RSPCA over animal welfare. It was Mr Clutterbuck's additional observation that raised eyebrows. 'I imagine now it would be illegal to only have animals of the opposite sex!' he wrote, and pressed 'Reply all'.

Naturally, the more sensitive councillors in a town with a large and thriving homosexual population quickly spotted the potential offence his comments might cause – and shopped him to the papers.

'I don't know whether I'm daft, but I still don't know what I have done to upset them so much', said Mr Clutterbuck in response to the subsequent furore. 'I have never even remotely done anything against anyone who was homosexual.' He added, 'It's absolute nonsense. I'm not apologizing. I have not done anything wrong.' When asked if he was homophobic, he replied firmly in the negative. 'I'm not homophobic at all, and I never have been.'

This admirable assertion was slightly muddied, however, by his later remarks. 'I was brought up as a Christian and have Christian beliefs, and I do think that certain things are wrong but these are my thoughts and I keep them to myself . . . As long as they do it behind closed doors I don't mind, but they [homosexuals] control the media, the television. They have much stronger control than they should have.'

Mr Clutterbuck was fired.

5 October

2006

Today a surgeon in Romania finally let all the stress he'd been suffering from get to him. Naum Ciomu expressed his frustration after making a mistake during a complex operation on 36-year-old Nelu Radonescu to correct a testicular problem. He chopped off Mr Radonescu's penis.

To make matters worse, he then placed the member on the operating table in front of shocked nursing staff and sliced it into small pieces before storming out of the building. The victim had to have reconstructive surgery using tissue from his arm.

Ciomu later admitted that he may have 'over-reacted'.

6 October

1992

There's always something satisfying about the hunters becoming the hunted, so it's understandable that the police in Newcastle upon Tyne were pleased with their thief-catching car the Rat Trap. This clever invention was a standard Ford Sierra saloon car with a few important modifications: doors that automatically locked, windows that couldn't be opened from the inside and an engine that cut out after twenty seconds. The theory was that if it was left on city streets known to be targeted by car thieves, they wouldn't be able to resist breaking in and would be trapped. It worked astonishingly well – no fewer then thirty-one would-be robbers were caught in eighteen months.

Then, suddenly, on this night in 1991, the car was stolen. 'There was a malfunction' was all that a police spokesman would say in explanation.

7 October

1986

The scheduled opening of a time capsule in Wilkinsburg, Pennsylvania, didn't happen today – or any day for the rest of the week during the town's centennial celebrations. The stainless-steel box had been hidden in 1962, and those in charge of the operation had wanted to keep its location secret to prevent vandals from digging it up. Sadly, however, by 1986 they had all passed away. Eighty-seven-year-old Harold Ake at least recalled that the City Council had held a special closed meeting to decide where they were going to put the capsule, adding, 'but they didn't tell anyone'.

8 October

1854

When Jim Kelly sent out a blanket invitation to his birthday party, news spread up and down the Barbary Coast like wildfire. The owner of one of the most notorious boarding houses in wild mid-nineteenth-century San Francisco was going to hire a steamboat and lay on free drinks and free women for all his guests, all night. Who wouldn't want to go to a bash like that?

Anyone with any sense is the answer. Because Jim Kelly's nickname was 'Shanghai Jim', and 'shanghai-ing' was the art of press-ganging unwilling men on to ships that needed crews. Kelly earned his alternative moniker by whacking people over the back of the head and bundling them on to boats or by mixing them his favourite cocktail (schnapps, beer and enough sleep-inducing opium to fell an elephant) and allowing them to wake from their stupor only when they were safely on board a boat they didn't want to be on.

Kelly had received a request from a ship that needed a full ninety men. Not coincidentally, that was the number of people that he allowed on to his party boat once those foolish enough to be tempted by his overtures arrived. Legend has it that, soon after the boat steamed off, it changed direction for the open sea – and there was no one conscious left to protest.

To make the event even more delicious for Jim Kelly, he returned to port a hero. On the way back to San Francisco his steamboat had come across the wreck of the *Yankee Blade,* and he picked up hundreds of survivors. So great was the excitement about this feat that hardly anyone noticed that his original cargo was missing . . .

The confused party-goers, meanwhile, woke up the next morning on board *The Reefer*, an infamous hell ship, notorious for working its crew literally to death, hundreds of miles from land and with no hope of getting back there for a very long time.

9 October

1999

A weekend hunting expedition in Finland proved more deadly for humans than it did for birds when a bullet pierced a grouse and then went on to hit the brother of the man who first fired the gun, more than a mile away. The hunter had aimed at the bird as it sat in a tree about 114 metres away, but the bullet kept on going and then struck the hunter's brother on its downward trajectory as he and friends were cooking sausages over a camp-fire.

10 October

1994

Robert Puelo was causing so much trouble in a store in St Louis that a clerk felt obliged to call the police. Puelo reacted angrily, grabbed a hot dog, stuffed it into his mouth and walked out without paying. When the police arrived, they found him unconscious just outside the door. Paramedics later removed the six-inch sausage from his throat. It had choked him to death.

11 October

1992

Kenneth Arrowood from Cleveland, Georgia, today lost his battle to sue his mother for $2,613. Arrowood, a car mechanic, had claimed that his mother owed him the money for repairs he had carried out on her pick-up truck. She counter-sued, however. In her suit the 78-year-old explained that 'the plaintiff is indebted to the defendant for forty years of services rendered as a mother, guidance counsellor, cook, maid, banker, nurse, bail bondswoman, babysitter, laundry worker and psychologist, all of which the plaintiff has not paid for'. Mrs Arrowood also recommended that the judge gave her son 'the whipping that he so rightly needs and which I failed to give him as a child'. The judge declined to whip Kenneth but did rule in his mother's favour.

12 October

1977

TV hypnotist Romark (also known, slightly more prosaically, as Ron Markham) had a mixed record of success and failure in his chequered career. As fans of Crystal Palace football club can unhappily attest, the curse he put on the team has been long and durable, but a similar attempt he once made to jinx a boxing match for Muhammad Ali can only be considered a partial success. The ring collapsed under Ali at the weigh-in, but he still went on to KO his opponent, Richard Dunn, in double-quick time.

The real low point in Romark's career, however (at least until he was arrested for stealing money from his mother when she lay in hospital), came when he declared that he was going to prove the extent of his psychic powers by driving a car blindfolded through Ilford.

An expectant crowd watched as he placed two coins over his eyes, held in place by a thick band and, oddly, a slice of dough. They gasped as he climbed into a yellow Renault and drove it off down the Cranbrook road. They laughed when twenty yards later he drove it into the back of a police van. 'That van', explained Romark, 'was parked in a place where logic told me it shouldn't be.'

13 October

1995

When stuck in a traffic jam, Michael Moreci, a prison guard from Illinois, decided to vent his frustration by revving his engine. When another driver asked him to stop, Moreci leaned out of his window and informed him that 'I beat up guys like you for a living'. Just for good measure, he added, 'Get out of the car and I'll leave you bloody in the street'. These were not sensible words. The other driver was a local judge, Sam Amirante. A $500 fine was slapped on to Moreci. Miraculously, however, he kept his job.

14 October

2000

Shortly before the millennium, the former rockabilly singer Buffalo Bill Hawkins (who has now changed his name to Yisrayl Hawkins) managed to convince some 3,000 people that he was a 'witness' who would announce Christ's second coming before being murdered by Satan and ushering in the end of the world in the year 2000. He and his followers hid out in an armed compound in scrublands near Abilene, Texas: a significant place according to Hawkins because, he says, if you travel west from the Abilene in Israel – the one mentioned in the Old Testament – you travel right through Abilene in Texas. This journey must be presumed to be miraculous, as the two places are on very different latitudes. Still the followers managed to build a 'holy city', where they could await the End of Days. 'Thankfully, we only have a year left of this madness', said Hawkins in 1999.

Of course, as it turned out, there was more than a year to go. This didn't perturb too many of Hawkins's followers, however – several hundred of whom had already demonstrated their devotion to their leader by changing their own surnames to 'Hawkins' in 1996. They even stayed with him when he once again mistakenly prophesied that the last three years of mankind's time on earth would commence on 14 October 2000, when nuclear bombs were due to block out the sun and wipe out 80 per cent of the human race within twelve months. That didn't happen either.

15 October

1987

'A woman rang and said she heard a hurricane is on the way', said British weatherman Michael Fish at the end of his forecast for the day. 'Well, if you are watching and waiting, there isn't.' Early the next morning the hurricane did in fact arrive. It was the biggest storm the UK had seen for three centuries. Thirteen people were killed, thousands of trees were destroyed and millions of pounds' worth of damage occurred.

16 October

2006

A family's enjoyment of a pizza meal in New Malden, south-west London, was considerably lessened when a total stranger walked up to their table and emptied a bag of urine over their heads and their food. Alex Giarola, the manager of the Pizza Piazza restaurant, told local paper the *Wimbledon Guardian* that 'the family were just having a good time and enjoying their meal before the guy walked in'.

The man, whom no one was able to identify, was heard to mutter 'This is for you' before throwing a clear plastic bag filled with urine over the family. The luckless diners then had to sit for thirty minutes in their dripping clothes and in front of their soggy pizzas while they waited for local police to arrive and investigate the bizarre crime scene.

The one silver lining in this otherwise far too cloudy day came when the restaurant decided to waive their bill. Mr Giarola explained: 'Of course we didn't charge the family for the meal; we just felt so sorry for them.'

2001

Security refused Bob Dylan entrance to the backstage area for one of his own concerts because he was not wearing a pass. With the heightened tension after the atrocity on 11 September, guards had strict orders from Dylan's security director that no one was to be allowed backstage without official accreditation. 'He said no exceptions', explained venue manager Chris Borovansky. 'Absolutely none.'

1986

The first UK royal tour of China was a big diplomatic event, especially since it came just one year before the controversial handover of Hong Kong from British to Chinese control. That seasoned traveller Prince Philip, the royal consort, was not overawed by the occasion, however. When he met a group of students from Edinburgh University, he chatted with them happily, quipping, 'If you stay here much longer, you will go back with slitty eyes'. He also tactfully remarked on what a 'ghastly' place Peking was and seemed to be just getting into his stride when, in the words of one student, 'his wife calmed him down'. The headline of the *Daily Mirror* the next day was 'The Great Wally of China'.

17 October

2006

When Henry Bingham wanted time off, he decided to tell his workmates that his two-year-old daughter had died. At first it worked. After he announced the sad news in a meeting on 16 October 2006, he was granted compassionate leave, his sympathetic colleagues clubbed together to give him more than $1,300 and the next day his labour union chipped in with some cash too.

The one thing that Bingham hadn't counted on was someone from his office in Wyoming telephoning his wife on the following day to offer condolences. That person was surprised to hear from her that the child was actually alive and well.

Bingham was quickly arrested by the local sheriff for obtaining property under false pretences – a charge with a maximum jail sentence of ten years. He told a sheriff's deputy that he made up the story to try to get time off from work, but, strangely, he was unable to explain why he had taken the money – and why, indeed, he had in fact continued to turn up at work.

1929

Irving Fisher, a respected US economist, was feeling bullish about affairs on Wall Street. 'Stock prices have reached what looks like a permanently high plateau', he wrote to the amusement of all posterity. 'I do not feel there will be soon, if ever, a 50 or 60 point break from present levels . . . I expect to see the stock market a good deal higher within a few months.'

A few days later share prices collapsed, and the Great Depression began.

18 October

2001

A drunk Norwegian who charged into a bank and handed over a note saying 'this is a robbery' thought he had done enough to conceal his identity by wearing a pair of underpants over his head. However, as he learned when police came and woke him up two days later, he'd made a very important mistake. He'd left his wife's name and address on the back of the note. The man later told the court that he had no recollection of carrying out the robbery, but that he had started getting a feeling he'd been misbehaving when he saw a picture of a man with a familiar-looking pair of knickers on his head in a local paper – and found a large pile of money in his living-room.

19 October

2001

Gary McGowan, a drink-driver who had abandoned his vehicle while fleeing police, thought that his luck was in when a car pulled up alongside him. 'Jump in mate', said a voice from inside the car, and young Gary did just that. He put his feet up on the dashboard and gave directions for his home. It was only when the driver told him he was under arrest that he realized he wasn't in a taxi at all. He was, in fact, in a police car. 'I was laughing so much that I could hardly put the cuffs on him', said arresting officer PC Stoker.

20 October

1988

According to Florida newspaper the *St Petersburg Times*, a falling dog caused three deaths in central Buenos Aires. The dog, a poodle named Cachi, fell, appropriately enough, from a thirteenth-floor balcony, hitting 75-year-old Marta Espina on the head. Both the animal and the old woman died instantly. A crowd gathered around the remarkable and bloody scene – and then Edith Sola, who was standing on its edge, was run over by a passing bus. An unidentified man who saw both accidents then entered cardiac arrest and died in the ambulance on the way to hospital. Police were unable to explain why the dog fell.

21 October

1999

Breatharians believe that it is possible to live on 'light' alone. They say that unpolluted air contains all the nutrients necessary to sustain life and that not eating food will actually increase a person's longevity. The spiritual diet's most well-known advocate is Ellen Greve, who says that she took up Breatharianism after she was 'told' to change her life by her spiritual mentor, St Germain, a Frenchman last seen living in the sixth century AD. Ellen also changed her name to the more mystical Jamuheen. In 1999 she made the remarkable claim that she'd spent the last six years living on nothing more than herbal tea and the odd chocolate biscuit. However, when the Australian TV programme *60 Minutes* challenged her to practise what she preached in front of TV cameras, she quickly became ill. Within forty-eight hours she was showing signs of serious dehydration. After four days she had lost a stone and, although she maintained that she felt 'really good', the experiment was cancelled today for health reasons.

Shortly after this monumentally bad piece of publicity Breatharianism received yet more unfavourable notices when another prominent advocate was filmed leaving a baker's shop tucking into a chicken pie. By the time a journalist reported he'd sat next to Jamusheen on a plane and claimed he'd heard her ordering a vegetarian meal (before realizing who he was and refusing to eat it), they were an international laughing-stock – albeit one with hundreds of starving followers.

22 October

2006

When his satellite navigation system told a German motorist to 'turn right now', he immediately obeyed. Thirty metres before the crossing he was supposed to take, he drove his sport utility vehicle off the road, on to a building site, up some stairs and into the side of a small toilet hut, much to the surprise of its occupants.

23 October

1999

Saliamin Akrami's last act on earth was to take a drunken wee on the track at Kensal Green railway station. His urine stream hit the live rail and, according to reports, '600 volts formed an arc into the tip of his penis'. The jury at the subsequent inquest recorded a verdict of 'death by misadventure'.

24 october

2006

Muradif Hasanbegovic embarrassed security officials at the prison that was supposed to be housing him when he climbed inside a box he had constructed and mailed himself to freedom.

Hasanbegovic worked in the prison workshop, where he packaged and posted parts for lampposts. Today he simply climbed inside a box he had made and got his fellow inmates to load him on to a lorry. 'I noticed the tarpaulin had a hole in it just as the prison called me and asked, "Have you noticed anything funny? We are kind of missing a prisoner" ', the truck driver told police. Stating the blindingly obvious, the warden said, 'this sort of thing was not supposed to happen'.

At the time of writing, Hasanbegovic has still not been found.

25 october

1993

Australian Laura McKenzie was a law-abiding motorist. So law-abiding, in fact, that when she got stuck at a malfunctioning red light on an isolated outback road, she didn't move for two whole days. She was eventually taken to hospital with dehydration, from where she commented: 'How was I supposed to know it was broken? It was red, so I just behaved properly.'

26 october

2002

At a large plumbing convention in Fort Worth, Texas, one of the attendees and his wife retired to use the facilities in their hotel room. Suddenly the toilet exploded, jettisoning its contents all over the alarmed couple.

'It was quite humorous because it happened to a consultant who was famous for conducting a study about exploding toilets', said Stanley Wolfson, the event planner for the American Society of Plumbing Engineers. 'I mean, really, what are you going to do if you can't laugh about an exploding toilet?' he added. 'Especially when it happens to a plumbing engineer.'

27 October

2000

John Robert Broos told police he was assaulted and robbed by two men outside the St Croix Casino in Turtle Lake, Wisconsin. He reported that the attack occurred just after 11 a.m., saying that he got out of his car and that then a hard object had hit him on the back of the head, he'd fallen to the ground and the $50 dollar bill he had brought with him to gamble in the casino had been stolen. He had some nasty bumps on the back of his head to prove it, along with dirt on his clothes and a cut on the left side of his face.

When police studied security tapes, however, they were surprised to see Broos arriving in the casino car park almost an hour earlier than he had stated. They were also confused when they saw footage of him entering the casino and emerging twenty minutes later with a thoughtful look on his face.

The mystery was cleared up when they next saw the luckless gambler hurling himself at a lamppost and smudging dirt into his cheeks. He then checked his reflection in his wing-mirror, and repeated the entire process, achieving a more than passable mugging-victim look, but unaware that a camera was trained on him the entire time. When satisfied with his handiwork, he went into the casino – where he had clearly just lost his $50 and reported the robbery.

'Unbelievable', said the director of surveillance at the casino. 'We get all kinds.'

28 october

2003

Cathy Ord and Rose Bucher weren't unduly put out when gun-wielding robber Alfred Joseph Sweet broke into their Florida home through their kitchen window. In fact, they were very nice to him. 'We just treated him with kindness', Bucher said later. They gave him a ham sandwich and invited him to take a shower and shave so that he would be less recognizable to police. They also handed him a bottle of rum, which Sweet tucked into with enthusiasm. After five hours of cosy chat and drinking Sweet nodded off in the comfy chair he was offered. He was still sleeping like a baby when the police came to arrest him.

29 october

1985

'I'm no linguist, but I have been told that in the Russian language there isn't even a word for freedom', said Ronald Reagan, but only the first part of his statement was correct. The Russian word for freedom is *svoboda*.

30 October

2005

The Revd Kyle Lake was performing a baptism in Waco, Texas. He was standing in the small pool used for baptisms in front of an 800-strong congregation when he reached out to adjust a nearby microphone, which produced a huge electric shock.

'At first, there was definitely confusion just because everyone was trying to figure out what was going on', Ben Dudley, a church pastor, told reporters. 'Everyone just immediately started praying.' Then Lake was taken by ambulance to a local medical centre, but he was pronounced dead on arrival.

Before this bizarre incident, Pastor Lake was best known as the author of a book entitled, with clanging irony, *Understanding God's Will*.

31 October

1992

When flares lit up the small island of Inchkeith on the Firth of Forth in Scotland, local coastguards watched but did nothing. 'The island is supposed to be connected with witchcraft', one explained, and went on to say that they just assumed that the fires and lights were part of some unholy Halloween ritual. In fact, the flares were a distress signal from a yacht, as the embarrassed coastguards realized when they received separate reports of its predicament. Fortunately, the lifeboat reached the site on time.

November

1 November

In an extraordinary piece of misfortune for the author of this book, nothing of note appears to have happened on this day at all. Or at least, nothing funny enough to note here. Indeed, my research suggests that this may well be the luckiest day of the year.

2 November

1995

Young Australian fisherman Adrian Bush wasn't catching enough fish – not according to his captain, Graham Griffin, anyway. That's why the skipper pushed him off the boat into a pack of sharks. Fortunately, Bush managed to climb back on board the boat without suffering serious external injury.

However, he claims never to have been the same since mentally, saying that he suffers a recurring nightmare, which is decidedly unsurprising in its content: 'Sharks. All you can see . . . is sharks thrashing around. You can't swim away', he told Australian Broadcasting.

3 November

1998

Daniel Hughes, a pet shop assistant in Paisley, Scotland, lost his job when he was discovered juggling. It wasn't so much the neglect of his duties that annoyed his employers as the fact that he was using three of the store's guinea pigs instead of balls.

4 November

1873

William Shanks published the fruits of the labours of the last twenty years of his life: 'On the Extension of the Numerical Value of *pi*', a paper in which he calculated the value of *pi* to 707 decimal places. Sadly, in 1944 D.F. Ferguson came along and proved that much of Shanks's work had been wasted. He had got the number at the 528th decimal place wrong, which meant that all his subsequent figures were therefore also incorrect. Ferguson had used a computer, and it took him mere months to prove Shanks wrong.

5 November

1985

Two-year-old Robyn Daigneault climbed inside the old-fashioned 35-inch-high milk can that her family used to collect pennies and refused to get out. Her four-year-old brother Roy raised the alarm with a lusty cry of 'Ma! Robyn's stuck in the penny bank', prompting many frustrating hours for the rest of the family as they tried to extract her. Even the promise of ice cream and lollipops failed to persuade the child to raise her arms so that she could be pulled up, and the canned infant was eventually carried to the local hospital.

There Dr Larry Proano toyed with the idea of using cutting torches and gallons of mineral oil to extract the youngster, but eventually opted to give her the experience of a second birth. He turned the can upside down while a nurse positioned himself underneath. Robyn's head popped out of the can and 'then we delivered the shoulders one at a time, just like a baby', Proano is reported to have said.

Following the heels of the two-year-old came more than two thousand pennies.

1605

Guy Fawkes's attempt to blow up the Houses of Parliament was foiled, and more than 300 MPs survived.

6 November

2004

Some Czech students were drunk. Realizing this fact, they thought it would be a good idea to have some coffee. As one of them explained to a Czech newspaper later: 'We grabbed the first tin we found, put what we thought was coffee in mugs and poured hot water over it.'

Apparently the drink didn't taste too good and seemed even a bit old, but as the same student said: 'We needed a drink to sober up and so we just downed it.' It was only when their host came into the room that the students discovered their mistake. 'You idiots,' he shouted at them, 'you've just drunk my grandfather's ashes.'

Naturally, this announcement had quite a sobering effect on the gathering, but fortunately, Jakub Havlat, the young descendant of the recently deceased and all too decaffeinated, was able to see the funny side. 'My grandfather had a great sense of humour, so he's probably laughing now', he said.

7 November

2002

There's no faulting the logic of the Iranian man who decided that robbing a bank would be far easier if he was invisible. There's also something admirable about his determination to carry his grand idea through to its conclusion. It's just a shame that reality intervened and destroyed his schemes.

During his trial our hapless anti-hero (whose name the Iranian courts declined to release) explained that he visited a 'sorcerer' on 7 November 2002, and parted with 5 million Rials (about £260) in exchange for a piece of paper that the sorcerer insisted would make him disappear.

Delighted, he tied the parchment around his arm and marched off to the nearest bank. He was surprised and disappointed, however, when, soon after he began snatching money out of customers' hands, they began pointing and shouting at him. He was devastated when they then overpowered him and handed him over to the police. 'I made a mistake. I understand now what a big trick was played on me', the all too visible man told the court.

The mysterious sorcerer has not been seen since.

1962

Richard Nixon lost the gubernatorial election in the US state of California. In his concession speech he stated that this was his 'last press conference' and that 'you won't have Dick Nixon to kick around any more'.

1972

Richard Nixon won the US Presidential election.

1872

The *Marie Celeste* set sail for the last time. The ship was next seen floating just off Portugal, entirely bereft of her crew. The missing men were never found – and the puzzle of how they disappeared has never been solved.

8 November

1993

Salvatore Chirilino, out walking in his favourite beauty spot in Vibo Marina, Italy, couldn't believe his luck when he saw a four-leaf clover. He told his wife that it meant this would be a very special day indeed. Then he slipped on the wet grass and plunged 150 feet to his death.

9 November

1995

Local councillor Billy Buchanan's meeting at Falkirk Town Hall got off to a poor start when the rumoured guest speaker failed to turn up. Because of his claims of intimacy with UFO phenomena and beings from outer space, locals had become convinced that Buchanan had invited Zal-us, a member of the Inter-Galactic Council of Nine, to talk at the event. As a consequence more than 700 punters packed into the hall, but surprisingly the benevolent extraterrestrial stayed away. Instead, they had to put up with a long speech from an American, who urged them to hug more trees. Buchanan resigned a few months later, citing 'stress' as the main reason for his decision.

10 November

1809

Theodore Hook was one of nineteenth-century London's most celebrated figures, the editor of the infamous satirical magazine *John Bull* and the best-selling novelist of his time before Dickens came along. However, it is as a brilliant practical joker that he is best remembered today, mainly thanks to the audacious trick he once played on the occupier of 54 Berners Street in central London.

54 Berners Street was actually an unprepossessing address. So modest, indeed, that Hook's friend (whom posterity remembers only as 'Beazley') remarked on how very ordinary it was, as the two men were walking past it one morning. Straight away Hook bet Beazley a guinea that he could make this house the most famous place in town within a week.

Hook quickly ascertained that the building's sole inhabitant was an elderly widow named Mrs Tottingham. Over the next few weeks he started sending out letters in her name inviting everyone he could think of to come and visit the poor old lady. He requested that surgeons came to cure her ills, sweeps to clean her chimneys and confectioners to bring her sweets. Among other things he ordered a keg of beer, several sacks of potatoes, tons of coal, wigs, a wedding cake, a hearse and even a church organ. In total, he sent out more than a thousand letters.

The trouble began at 9 a.m. on 10 November, when a confused Mrs Tottingham turned away a coalman who claimed to have an order of coal for her that she could not remember placing. Soon Berners Street was in absolute chaos.

The Duke of York arrived too, having being informed that one of his 10,000 men lay dying in 54 Berners Street. Following swiftly behind him came the chairman of the East India Company, the Duke of Gloucester, the Archbishop of Canterbury and even the Mayor of London, in his state carriage.

It was the Mayor who finally managed to disperse the huge crowd, which had by then completely blocked the street and surrounding area. Apparently, this eminent functionary had fallen victim to a similar prank from Hook in the past, and he was immediately suspicious. He managed to disperse the crowds but was unable to prove any charges against Hook, who had hidden his traces with consummate skill. Had he looked across the street, however, he might have seen the joker and his friend Beazley laughing hysterically from a neighbour's window at the trouble they had caused.

1953

Dylan Thomas, the Welsh poet, died. His last words are widely thought to have been: 'I've had eighteen straight whiskies; I think this is a record.' However, his friend Heliker claims he slipped in another few words after this famous utterance: 'After thirty-nine years, this is all I've done.'

11 November

1993

Using a cigarette lighter, three-year-old Mikey Sproul from Tampa, Florida, burned down his family home, sending his father to hospital with severe burns in the process. 'Now I have no house', he correctly told reporters. The press had been especially keen to hear the precocious infant's remarks after this event because just over a month earlier, on 1 October, he had made national news by making off in his family car and driving it down a major highway, only coming to a halt after he hit two parked cars. His summary back then? 'I go zoom.'

12 November

2006

Staff at the Holiday Inn in West Point, Mississippi, were surprised when twenty-year-old Kevin Pugh walked into the reception and threw a 60-pound pig over the counter.

No one was hurt (and the pig was fine), officers said, but a considerable amount of police time was used up because three other disturbances took place at local businesses between 2 a.m. and 4 a.m. One other pig was tossed, and there were two further incidents involving possums. 'This was the silliest thing I've ever seen', said police lieutenant Danny McCaskill. 'Almost every officer we had was involved because the incidents kept happening at different hours.'

Kevin Pugh was eventually fined the strangely specific sum of $279, but police remained baffled by his actions. 'It must be some redneck thing', explained McCaskill.

1970

An 8-ton sperm whale was discovered rotting on a beach in Oregon. The local highway division decided that the best way to dispose of the corpse would be to remove it the same way they did a boulder – and blow it up with explosives. They used half a ton of dynamite. The resulting blast covered the seventy-five spectators (including several bemused local newsmen) in whale fat. More than a quarter of a mile from the beach, a parked car was severely dented by pieces of flying blubber. Most of the whale remained in one piece, however, and was left for workers from the highway division to clear away.

13 November

1987

The day after winning $50,000 on a televised lottery show in West Virginia, Clarence Kinder dropped dead of a heart attack.

14 November

2005

In an attempt to break a world record, staff from Endemol TV had set up more than 4 million dominoes in a building in Leeuwarden in the Netherlands. Security was ultra-tight because the excellently named local radio DJ Ruud de Wild had offered a 3,000 Euro reward to anyone who could knock the dominoes over before the start of the event. Not one person managed to break into the building, but calamity struck anyway. A sparrow flew in through a window and landed on the domino run, causing 23,000 dominoes to fall down before built in gaps stopped the collapse. It was a bad day for the bird too, because an exterminator then tracked it down and shot it – much to the outrage of animal rights activists.

15 November

1997

A Vietnamese husband came to regret sneaking up on his wife and tickling her as she chopped firewood when she instinctively hurled the axe she was using at her tormentor. It nearly decapitated him, and he died shortly afterwards. The woman, 62-year-old Siek Phan, explained to the authorities who arrested her, 'I hate being tickled'.

16 November

1988

The Agave Americana is a South American plant much prized by botanists and is especially hard to cultivate in the British climate. Norton nurseries in Sheffield were therefore justly proud of their 25-foot specimen, which had survived fifty winters, not to mention the Second World War. What's more, 1988 was an extra-special year for this particular plant because it was beginning to develop a flower – something that the species does just once every fifty to a hundred years in the UK. Today the little bud was just beginning to open up when a council workman accidentally reversed his lorry on to the plant and crushed it.

17 November

1983

Jimmy 'The Beard' Ferrozzo met his untimely end in a San Francisco strip bar when he was crushed between a grand piano and a 12-foot-high ceiling.

The trick piano had been part of the act of the entertainer Carol Doda for almost twenty years. Carol had used it to make her entrance, reclining across the instrument's shiny black surface as it was lowered from the ceiling by a cable. On that fateful November night, however, Ferrozzo had been using it for his own purposes, as was demonstrated by the fact that beneath his prone body rescuers found a naked and hysterical dancer called Teresa Hill.

Rescuers surmised that she and Ferrozzo must have kicked the switch that raised the piano to the ceiling while in the throes of passion. Apparently the instrument's ascent was slow and gradual, but the couple were so intent on their amours that they didn't notice their unusual change in circumstances until it was too late. Ferrozzo probably saved Hill's life with a last-second kick that cut the switch on the motorized piano hoist. The cushioning effect of his body prevented her from being crushed, while he himself died from asphyxiation. It took the fire department almost three hours to pry the couple loose.

Hill was said to have been so intoxicated that she couldn't remember how she had ended up in such an unusual position. 'She just remembers waking up and being pinned to the piano', said the detective on the scene, Guinther Whitey.

1973

'I'm not a crook', declared Richard Nixon to the world's media in relation to the Watergate scandal. The words would come back to haunt him less than a year later, when it became clear that he had orchestrated the break-in at Democratic Party headquarters in the Watergate hotel in Washington – and the subsequent cover-up. 'I was not lying. I said things that later seemed to be untrue', explained the ex-President.

18 November

2006

A Serbian prisoner granted weekend release chose the wrong house to burgle – the one belonging to his prison governor. Alija Cerimi's crime was detected when he returned to prison in the northern town of Sremska Mitrovica, and the governor spotted that he was wearing his watch. According to witnesses, the enraged official shouted 'That's mine, you thieving bastard!' before ordering guards to restrain the luckless criminal.

19 November

1866

Any audience prepared to go to a seven-and-a-half-hour play has to be considered relatively hardy, but even those brave souls who ventured out for the one and only performance of Edward Falconer's *Lovers of Lismona* were not up to the unique challenges his work presented. Theatre critics reporting on this memorable event noted that by 11 p.m. (just three and a half hours into the performance) most of the audience were sleeping. By midnight, most of the audience had left. At 2 a.m. just a handful of slumbering critics remained, and it was clear that the play was going to overrun its time dramatically. The stage hands took a vote and, for the sake of audience and actors alike, lowered the curtain. The play still hasn't been performed in its entirety.

20 November

1993

Two days before the thirtieth anniversary of the Kennedy assassination, when graphic footage of the President's death dominated the US media, Dale Christensen, an Illinois football coach, hit on a great scheme to inspire his team before a crucial match. He would arrange for a fake shooting – of himself – in the cafeteria where his team were eating their pre-match snacks.

The basic scheme was that he would appear to go over and break up an argument, someone would pull a gun on him and then he'd collapse to the ground, apparently dead. Thanks to this shocking event, he reasoned, his team would be horrified, enraged and overflowing with adrenalin. All this righteous anger would then be channelled into the joyous desire to wreak havoc on the football field when they then saw their heroic coach get up from the floor, as if from the dead, and tell them to go out and kick butt.

Everything went according to plan. He was shot. He fell. Fake blood oozed from his chest. He got up again and gave his high-energy pep talk . . .

The only trouble was that the highly traumatized team went out and received a thumping – their first defeat in twelve games. In his resignation message coach Christensen described the fiasco as 'a lesson plan that went awry'.

1980

'I've talked to you on a number of occasions about the economic problems our nation faces, and I am prepared to tell you, it's in a hell of a mess . . . We're not connected to the press room yet, are we?'

So asked US President Ronald Reagan. The answer, of course, was 'Yes, we are'.

21 November

1980

On this misty autumnal dawn at Lake Peigneur in Louisiana all was quiet. The only sound disturbing the piece of this local beauty spot (the home of Jackson Island and its renowned Live Oak Gardens botanical park) was the steady throbbing of the oil drills that lined the lake's perimeter.

Suddenly, at 6.30 a.m. one of the oil platforms started to tilt. Then, just as platform crews made it to the lakeshore, the waters of Peigneur started to turn. A giant whirlpool formed before the amazed eyes of the workers, and the lake drained away into a hole in the lake-bed like bathwater going down a plughole.

Soon almost the entire lake had disappeared, together with two Texaco drilling rigs, 70 acres of Jackson Island, several greenhouses, five lakeside homes, a caravan, a few trucks and tractors, a car park, three dogs, a tugboat and eleven barges from an adjoining canal, which by then had changed direction and was also emptying itself into the crater, creating the largest waterfall in the state of Louisiana in the process.

The exact cause of this bizarre incident isn't certain, because most of the evidence was washed away along with the rest of the lake. What is clear, however, is that a Texaco drill had managed to break through into a large salt-mine that ran beneath the water, and the small hole had rapidly become a vast cavern as the mine's salt dissolved.

Miraculously, no one was killed. Fifty workers in the salt-mine had a lucky escape. A fishing trip was also brought to an abrupt end when the anglers' boat hit the mud at the bottom of the lake, two men still sitting in it, rods dangling uselessly over the side.

Texaco were left with a multi-million-pound bill, the mine was permanently closed and the Peigneur changed from an 11-foot-deep freshwater to a 1,300-foot-deep saltwater lake. Not all was lost, however, as the next day, in yet another bizarre twist, eleven of the sunk boats popped out on the surface like corks and were found floating on the now brackish water.

22 November

1667

The Revd Arthur Coga became a blood transfusion pioneer, voluntarily allowing members of the Royal Society in England to swap some of his own supply with 12 ounces of sheep's blood. The Revd Coga received, as the diarist Samuel Pepys recorded, just 20 shillings for his trouble – money he probably would have forsaken if scientists knew then what we know now about the importance of blood-type compatibility.

Pepys was pleased to note that he came across Coga alive and well a few days after the operation. 'He speaks well,' wrote the diarist, 'saying that he finds himself much better since, and as a new man.' Pepys remained sceptical, however, also noting that Coga was 'cracked a little in the head'. His pessimism was proved well founded when Coga dropped dead a few hours later.

23 November

2000

Goran Ivanisevic today crashed out of the Samsung Open tennis tournament when he smashed all three of his rackets in fits of temper and was unable to continue playing, owing to his self-imposed lack of equipment. 'At least when I've finished playing tennis, they'll remember me for something', Ivanisevic said sadly. 'They'll say, "There's that guy who never won Wimbledon, but he smashed all his rackets".'

Happily, less than a year later, the fiery Croat finally won Wimbledon.

1996

Ali Dia today made his first and only appearance on *Match of the Day* playing in the English football premiership.

Up until a few months previously, this young man from Senegal had been an undistinguished player for the undistinguished team Blyth Spartan. His fate had changed when the manager of the much bigger Southampton football club, Graeme Souness, received a call from someone claiming to be George Weah, the Liberian international and former Footballer of the Year. He told Souness to look out for Dia, saying that he was a Senegalese international of outstanding talent. This call was followed by another, purportedly from the legendary French international David Ginola, who persuaded Souness to sign Dia sight unseen.

So it was that Blyth Spartan's manager was amazed to see his old worst player on television as he was substituted on to the pitch 32 minutes into a game against Leeds Utd. Dia did his best to keep out of the action and thus avoid displaying his manifest lack of skill, but before long the player was left in front of an open goal – and managed to miss. Souness realized the extent of his error and called him off. It later became clear that Dia had never played for Senegal and was actually a mature student taking a course in business studies at Newcastle University.

'I don't feel I have been duped in the slightest', said Souness afterwards. 'That's just the way the world is these days.' Dia's manager at Blyth Spartan refused to criticise his former player either. 'At least he played in the Premiership,' he said, 'which is more than I ever did.'

24 November

1997

On this hot Monday morning in 1997 Bhagwanrao Raut, a Bombay construction worker, discovered that the argument he had had the day before with his colleague Vinayak Kadam was not yet over. He was brought to this understanding when Kadam approached him, whispered obscenities about his wife into his ear – and then bit if off.

'He said he ate the ear for fun', a bemused local policeman later explained, still sweating after the six hours he had spent with the fire brigade trying to persuade Kadam to come down from the perch in a tree where he had subsequently taken refuge.

1859

Charles Darwin published *The Origin of the Species*. One reviewer declared it 'so turgid, repetitive and full of nearly meaningless tables that it will only be read by specialists'. Leading British geologist Adam Sedgwick told the bearded author, 'I laughed . . . till my sides were sore'. Darwin had the last laugh, however. The book sold 1,250 copies on the first day alone and has never gone out of print. It has also raised some controversy, and even today the theories are not accepted in backward parts of Borneo, rural Pakistan, the USA and the UK.

25 November

1998

A sheep called Skaap gained celebrity status in her native South Africa when she adopted an orphaned baby elephant from the wild. She brought the elephant up and shared a shed with him, as well as nearly every waking moment. Tragically, this unlikely friendship was brought to an end on this day in 1998, when the elephant – known to his keepers as Jubulani – sat on his surrogate mother and she died of a heart attack.

'He seems OK now, but he was very quiet for the first couple of days after the incident', said Peter Rogers, a keeper at the

Hodespruit Breeding and Research Centre for Endangered Species, a few weeks after the accident occurred. 'He was gradually becoming more independent of the sheep anyway', he added.

1997

In Kuala Lumpur, Malaysia, golf novice Anthony Phua walked too close to his partner and was knocked out by his backswing. He got up immediately, apologized for getting in the way, collapsed again and died.

1997

Aimee Stone of Salt Lake City, Utah, died after falling head first into a vat of salsa.

26 November

2004

When Kevin Winston's daughter arrived home at 2.45 a.m. blind drunk, he was furious. So furious that he decided to teach her a lesson and call the police.

His plan backfired, however, when the wily child trumped him. Instead of getting upset when the police arrived, she led them to her father's stash of illegal narcotics and weapons, taking them up to the attic and on to a secret space in the roof, where surprised officers found four semi-automatic guns, including an AK-47 complete with banana clip, a sawn-off shotgun, a 9 mm handgun, a .22 calibre rifle, and more than 70 rounds of ammunition. Alongside this arsenal there were also 617 vials of cocaine.

Mr Winston was arrested and charged with three counts of possession of a high-capacity magazine, possession of assault weapons while in commission of drug-related crimes, possession of a controlled dangerous substance, possession with the intent to distribute, and drug possession within 1,000 feet of a school. His daughter just got a bad hangover.

27 November

2006, 2002, 1953, 1934, 1703, 1095

Although the superstitious would tell you that Friday 13th is the unluckiest day of the year, statistics suggest that this honour should actually go elsewhere. A study in 2006 by a group of UK insurers discovered that (for some unknown reason) 27 November is the real danger day.

Kevin Sinclair, of AA Insurance, said, 'Friday 13th is associated with bad luck, but you're more likely to have an accident on 27 November'. His claim is backed up by a litany of tales of woe from the cat who last year set a house on fire by knocking over a candle right back to the declaration of the disastrous First Crusade in 1095 via 'the great storm' of 1703, the fatal shooting of Al Capone's cohort Baby Face Nelson in 1934 and the 2002 car crash that hospitalized ageing Hollywood diva Zsa Zsa Gabor. He might also have added the 1953 death of the writer Eugene O'Neill. 'I knew it. I knew it', complained the writer. 'Born in a hotel room and – God damn it – died in a hotel room.'

28 November

1998

Disputes over karaoke microphones are never pretty at the best of times, but when they take place in a country awash with weapons left over from civil war and strife, things can get very nasty indeed.

On this night in 1998 in Cambodia two drunken soldiers were having such a good time blasting out their favourites that they refused to give up the microphone to another table. When a waitress insisted that their turn was over, one of the men became enraged – so enraged that he stormed into the back of the parlour, grabbed an axe and returned to smash the microphone into small pieces.

Naturally, the destruction of the microphone did not please the three men, who were still waiting to use it. So they pushed back their chairs, pulled out their automatic weapons and mowed down both soldiers in a hail of bullets.

29 November

2006

A man realized that his decision to go and smoke crack in what he thought was a quiet park in the Lakeland region of Florida was a mistake when an alligator grabbed him and tore off his left arm. Forty-five-year-old Adrian Apgar was pulled from the jaws of the beast at 4 a.m. on this day in 2006.

The unfortunate drug-user lost his left arm in the attack and suffered severe injuries to his right arm and left leg. As well as being high on crack, he was also 'totally naked', as local sheriff Grady Judd revealed to bemused local journalists.

The exact sequence of events is unclear. Apgar claims to have passed out on a beach in Lakeland shortly after finishing off the contents of his pipe, but after that, naturally enough, everything became hazy for the poor fellow.

What is known is that local man Carlos Mayid heard Apgar's anguished cries for help and called 911 from his mobile phone. While still talking to the 911 operator, Josh Fulman, he also got as close as he could to Apgar in order to try and reassure him that help was coming and to see if there was anything he could do.

He was unable to approach the alligator, but about five minutes into the nearly eight-minute call Fulman suggested that Mayid should tell Apgar to punch the toothy reptile. 'I don't know if it's true, but if you punch him in the nose . . . it may let him go', Fulman said. Mayid relayed the message and immediately came back with Apgar's response: 'Too big.' Mayid then informed Fulman, 'He says he needs a gun'.

Eventually the local sheriff and his deputies arrived on the scene. It was too dark and dangerous to get a shot in, so the brave men started to wrestle physically with the enraged alligator. 'We were pretty much playing tug-of-war', said a deputy.

Apgar was finally extricated and rushed to hospital in a critical condition. A bad day for Apgar turned out to be even worse for the 12-foot alligator, which was shot.

30 November

1900

Oscar Wilde, aged just forty-one, died in tragic circumstances in Paris after being hounded out of London society because of his sexual preferences, with his career and reputation seemingly ruined. At least his sense of humour still remained intact, as was proved by his last words: 'Either that wallpaper goes or I do.'

1016

Today, Edmund II 'Ironside', the king of England, was quite literally toppled from the throne. There are two legends relating to his untimely death, and both are equally painful.

The first story has it that he was killed by the son of Lord Edric Streona. The treacherous Streona had realized that Cnut Sveisson (later King Canute) had the upper hand in the invasion he had just launched on English shores, and so he had decided to win his favour by getting rid of the unlucky Edmund. To achieve this end, Edric placed his boy in the pit of the primitive royal outhouse and instructed him to stab the king in the bowels when he retired there to vacate them.

The other version is that the king was killed by an early remote-control weapon. Edric is said to have equipped his son with an ingenious device that caused a crossbow bolt to be fired up from the hole under the royal commode when the king sat on it. The agile boy simply set it up and let it do its work.

Either way, Edmund II received a nasty blow to his nether regions and died shortly afterwards.

Edric's fate wasn't much happier. When he ran to Cnut to boast of his achievement, the future king promised, 'I will exalt you higher than all the nobles of England!' He then had Edric's head chopped off and placed on a long pole on the highest battlement of his castle.

December

1 December

2003

A vicar in Germany had ordered 300 copies of a film of the life of Christ. Frithjof Schwesig, the pastor of the south-western town of Lampoldshausen, aimed to bring his fervent evangelical message into the homes of even those parishioners who didn't like to read. But his plan was foiled by a mix-up at the factory, which sent him hardcore porn movies instead of the religious epics he'd hoped for. He distributed them to about 300 people before he discovered their true nature.

Schwesig claimed not to have been too upset by the mistake, perhaps because only five of his parishioners are said to have complained about the distinctly blue movies. 'God moves in mysterious ways', he said cheerily a few days later, noting how much publicity the whole saga had gained for his little church. 'Best of all,' he added, 'the people who ordered the porn now have our religious films about Jesus in their video recorders.'

1135

King Henry I of England died, famously, of 'a surfeit of lampreys'. Apparently he was served a dish of the fish that was past its best-before date and expired within hours of eating them.

2 December

2005

Jessica Sandy Booth was a very pretty girl. Pretty enough to be a model in fact. The only thing holding her back was the fact that she needed $7,900 to pay a modelling agency to set up her portfolio.

When she was at an acquaintance's house and saw four men standing around a huge lump of a mysterious white substance sitting on a table, Jessica thought Christmas had come a few weeks early and her troubles were over. Her devious plan was to hire a hit man, get him to kill all the men in the house and take what was clearly thousands of dollars' worth of cocaine. Ruthlessly ambitious, she even told the hit man that if there were any witnesses – even children – he should kill them too.

We know that detail because it was caught on tape. Unbeknown to Jessica, the hit man she'd been hooked up with was an undercover cop. Even worse, when police went round to the house to search for the drugs, they discovered that rather than valuable narcotics, the men had actually been admiring a large lump of crumbly white cheese.

3 December

2006

A twelve-year-old boy in South Carolina was arrested for opening his Christmas presents too early. According to his mother, this act was the last straw after a long line of offences including habitual rudeness and petty theft. She reached the end of her tether when, in spite of being told not to, he opened his Game Boy Advance weeks early.

'He took it without permission. He wanted it. He just took it', explained the child's 63-year-old great-grandmother.

When the mother threatened to call the police, the youngster went into his room and got the Game Boy. So she called his bluff and invited the police to come over. Her plan backfired, however, because, she said, the boy showed 'no remorse' when the police took him away. What's more, he positively relished the subsequent media attention.

Arresting officer Lieutenant Jerry Waldrop, who gave the boy a good talking to but didn't take him to jail, later provided a neat summation of the incident. 'Yeah,' he said, 'it was strange.'

4 December

2006

The staff Christmas party at Santa's Magical Animal Kingdom in Mullingar, Ireland, was called off when one of the prize exhibits, Gus the camel, broke out of his pen and ate all the food. Once all the humans had gone home late on the Sunday night before the big event, Gus seized the opportunity presented by an unsecured gate on his pen and nudged his way out to freedom. He sauntered over to the table all spread out for the festivities and proceeded to eat his way through it.

He was discovered early the next morning, surrounded by detritus, having eaten over 200 mince pies and drunk a healthy six cans of Guinness. This latter feat impressed Clodagh Cleary, one of Santa's little helpers in the Magical Animal Kingdom, no end. 'He was biting the tops off with his big strong teeth and sucking the Guinness off the table like a man possessed', she told a reporter from the *Sunday Telegraph*. 'It was brilliant.'

1995

Bob Metcalfe, the founder of the 3Com Corporation, was confident of his knowledge of new technologies. For instance, when he wrote in a column that the internet would 'go spectacularly supernova and in 1996 catastrophically collapse', he promised to eat his words if he was proved wrong.

Early in 1997, in front of a large audience, Metcalfe put the 4 December 1995 column into a blender, poured in water and ate the resulting mixture with a spoon.

1980

Stella Walsh, the top female sprinter of the 1930s and multiple Olympic gold medal winner, was shot dead, an innocent victim of an armed robbery in Cleveland, Ohio. This tragic event was given added significance when a subsequent autopsy revealed that Stella was a fella and possessed male genitalia.

5 December

2006

Calvin E. Fluckes Jr chose precisely the wrong day to try to rip off a store in Chesterfield Township, Michigan. The signs were all there to warn him too. First of all, he should probably have noticed the forty marked police cars in the car park right next to the spot he chose. Second, if he'd been more alert, the large signs in the supermarket advertising a 'shop with a cop' event might have given him reason at least to delay his criminal undertaking. And if that didn't work, the presence of more than eighty uniformed cops in the shop should probably have made him turn back. But he didn't. Instead he tried to pay for $847.33 worth of goods with a poorly photocopied cheque and was almost instantaneously arrested. 'I can't even imagine what he was thinking', said police lieutenant David Marker.

1997

Alan Hall was found writhing in agony on his brother's front lawn. Near to him was his penis, which had been cut off at the base. Hall initially told investigating officers that the penis had been severed by an attacker called 'Brenda', who wanted revenge for a murder he had committed back in 1993. Later he bashfully admitted that he had actually cut off the organ himself while intoxicated, thinking that surgeons would easily be able to reattach it. Annoyingly for Mr Hall, that assumption was incorrect, and surgeons were unsuccessful in their attempts to make him whole again.

Further compelling proof of the universe's malign sense of humour came when it was revealed that Mr Hall is a pipe fitter by trade.

6 December

1911

Herr Teicht was a German tailor of considerable skill, but it's not his clothes he's remembered for as much as the large bat cape he constructed in 1911. He was convinced that this cleverly constructed item would give him the power to fly, enabling him to swoop gently to the ground from a great height with the grace of an eagle.

Accordingly, he applied to the management of the Eiffel Tower in Paris to test his invention, and incredibly they agreed, provided they were absolved of all responsibility and he obtained permission from the police. This last hurdle overcome, he took his cape to the first floor of the tower on this sunny December morning, leaped elegantly from the viewing platform to the admiring gasps of the gathered well-wishers and photographers and fell straight to the pavement below, where he was killed on impact.

7 December

2000

Claire Swire today became one of the world's first and biggest internet phenomena when her message to a male acquaintance,

Bradley Chait, reached millions of e-mail inboxes within hours of its initial sending.

The message in question followed on from an off-colour joke about 'swallowing' that Ms Swire sent to a few friends. Bradley replied to Claire individually, with a little gentle flirting, and soon they were on to the subject of her own technique and a night of intimacy they had recently enjoyed together. Claire said, famously, 'I hadn't swallowed for years, but yours was yum and very good for me too! Apparently it's very good conditioner for your hair too . . . getting a funny picture in my head, giggling out loud and now having to explain to Dave what's so funny!'

Unsurprisingly, Bradley was pleased and decided to forward the message on to a few friends. 'Now THAT'S a nice compliment from a lass, isn't it?' His friends were impressed. 'Beggars belief', wrote one, as he forwarded it on to another dozen acquaintances. 'I feel honour-bound to circulate this.'

It's since been calculated that the e-mail reached a million in-boxes within three hours, and countless more over the next couple of days. Sadly, some of those in-boxes belonged to Bradley Chait's employers, who disciplined him for misuse of the office e-mail. Claire Swire was forced into hiding, and very little has been heard from her since, although her name has entered the annals of internet legend.

8 December

2001

A retired nurse learned the hard way why it's never a good idea to irritate your dentist. She first visited David Quelch's dental practice in September and was so dissatisfied with the treatment she received there that she complained to her doctor. Oddly, however, she went to see Quelch again today and even informed him of the complaint she had made.

She described what happened next at a misconduct hearing of the UK General Dental Council: 'He told me he was going to extract my teeth. I objected, I didn't think it was necessary. He ignored my remarks and pulled out the tooth. I was bleeding profusely.' She added, 'I said I didn't want my tooth removed, [but] he pushed me back, pushing me hard across my chest and extracted the second tooth.'

'That'll teach you not to complain to the doctor about me!' Mr Quelch is then said to have shouted, while the blood was still pouring out of the patient's mouth.

At the disciplinary hearing Mr Quelch was struck off the record and banned from ever practising dentistry again. But that was scant compensation to his elderly victim for the loss of her teeth. 'All I wanted was a filling', she explained sadly.

9 December

1994

Late on this Friday, Moira Poor entered the lift in Auckland City Council's car park. She didn't leave it until sixty-seven hours later. She became the realization of every claustrophobic's worst nightmare when the faulty elevator got stuck between two floors and she was trapped alone with nothing more than her handbag. The alarm wasn't working, there was no phone and no one heard her cries for help . . . until 12 December.

10 December

1995

Scott Plumley was so annoyed when police told him that they didn't have enough evidence to shut down a dealer selling drugs in his neighbourhood in Pensacola, Florida, that he marched around to the dealer's house, bought a $4 bag of marijuana and phoned the police again to let them know what he had done. This time the police took action right away. They came around and arrested the unfortunate Mr Plumley. 'It is illegal to buy drugs for whatever reason', said a spokesman.

1994

Moira Poor spent today stuck in a lift.

11 December

2006

When Eloise D. Reaves was sold some ineffective crack cocaine, she was furious. Things were only going to get worse for her too, thanks to her subsequent decision to take her complaint about the low quality of the merchandise she had purchased to the nearest police officer.

The North Carolina woman approached the soon-to-be-bemused Deputy Jeffrey Pedrick as he worked a call at a shop in Putnam County, Florida. She informed him that a man in the nearby car park had sold her 'bad crack', removed a rock of the drug from her mouth and placed it on the boot of the policeman's car.

He told her that, if the substance tested positive for cocaine, he would have to arrest her. She told him it was wax and cocaine mixed, and that she wanted the Deputy to make the man in the car park give her money back.

The test did indeed test positive, and Reaves was booked into the Putnam County Jail. Her chagrin was only increased when Deputy Pedrick approached the man whom she had accused of selling her the dodgy drugs, searched him and found nothing at all incriminating on his person.

1994

Moira Poor also spent today stuck in a lift.

12 December

1994

Although poor old Moira Poor (*see* 9, 10, 11 December) was freed of her lift early this morning, her ordeal wasn't quite over.

After her rescuers had made sure she was all right and provided her with food and water, she made her way back to her vehicle and the car park exit. On the way out the attendant refused to believe her story, made her pay the full parking fee and then told her that she stank and that she should be ashamed to be out in public in the condition she was in.

The story did at least have a happy ending. Auckland City Council paid her £2,100 compensation and gave her free parking in Auckland for life.

1913

Emperor Menelik II of Ethiopia, suffering from severe ill health, became convinced that he could stave off death by eating pages from the Bible. With neat final irony he died of a stroke while masticating on the Book of Kings.

13 December

2004

When police pulled over a car that had just executed a slow-motion crash into a wall in a supermarket car park in Hamilton, New

Zealand, they weren't surprised to find that its two passengers were drunk. They were quite shocked, however, when the driver emerged and it became clear that he was almost completely blind.

Te Aute Matuakore, a 29-year-old musician with only 5 per cent vision, told police that he had decided to take over the vehicle when he realized that his two friends were too inebriated to handle it. His sozzled companions had then attempted to guide him into the car park – with one giving directions and the other holding on to the wheel. Sadly their valiant efforts to get the car off the road had been foiled, first by a sign and then by the wall which finally brought the vehicle to a halt.

The driver was made to pay $130 court costs and (hopefully superfluously) banned from driving for two years.

1958

Gordo the monkey, the first primate to be sent more than a mile into space, met his end when the parachute attached to the rocket cone that contained him failed to open and he crashed into the sea.

14 December

2000

The end-of-term prank pulled by four boys at Thorpe House public school in Buckinghamshire, England, came perilously close to sparking off an international incident. The boys had started off innocently enough by e-mailing the White House to wish Bill Clinton a Happy Christmas. Soon, however, they had egged themselves on to rather naughtier things.

'Send me a million dollars or I will blow up the White House', wrote one of the boys. Half an hour later he sent a yet more worrying message: 'I have not received my million dollars. It is now $2 million or I will blow up Texas.'

Computer whizzes at the FBI quickly tracked down the source of the threat and alerted Scotland Yard. Within minutes of the second e-mail being sent, the boy's headmaster received a phone call from Scotland Yard's Special Branch. Meanwhile, the boys received an automated e-mail response thanking them for contacting the President.

15 December

1995

Anne Osinga, the chairperson of a bird protection society in the Netherlands, was taken to hospital with concussion and a broken cheekbone after a dead goose plunged 75 feet from the sky and hit him on the head.

16 December

1916

Rasputin, the famous 'mad monk', Russian mystic and huge influen on the last Czar of Russia, today met his end. According to legend, aristocratic killers first tried to persuade him to eat cakes laced cyanide. Although there was said to be enough poison in the f have killed ten men, Rasputin showed no ill effects, either bec was sensible enough not to eat the deadly pastries or, as so have it, because of his supernaturally strong constitution.

That he was a tough old rogue was further evide events that followed. First Felix Lusparov, one of the p sins, shot Rasputin in the back. The monk fell, and him. Lusparov soon returned, however, realizing th coat behind. When he went for one last look at his victim's body, it woke up. Rasputin grabbed the surprised nobleman and began to throttle him. Just as Lusparov was beginning to fear for his own life, the monk released his neck, whispered (strangely) 'you bad boy' in his ear and fled the room.

While he was escaping, however, the rest of the party returned and shot Rasputin three times. He fell but continued to struggle, so they began to club him. They beat him viciously until they were convinced he must be dead, wrapped him in a sheet and threw him into the icy River Neva. Three days later the shot, poisoned and beaten body of Rasputin was found and an autopsy was carried out. The cause of death was discovered to be drowning.

17 December

2003

Bill Henderson's attempt to get the ultimate high by sitting himself ~he blending-room of a glue factory and turning off the exhaust ~s inspired but ultimately foolish. The lack of ventilation did ~t the room was filled with noxious fumes, but it also put ~mewhat off-balance. His plan came unstuck (ahem) ~ver a 500-gallon vat of contact cement, slipped ground.

~ in my life, but this guy takes the cake', said ~cosity tester at the Durable Fit Glue who was among the workers who ~er. She explained that he was ~d so firmly attached to the ~vels and a crowbar while ~at they might hurt him. ~er-glue his mouth shut and ~ift', said the unsympathetic

18 December

2006

A cattle rustler near the Russian port of Kaliningrad was caught trundling away from the scene of his crime – complete with several tons of live prize beef stock – in a bus. The Moscow news reported that police caught the man (whose name was not released) red-handed, in transit, with five confused-looking cows. He later explained that he thought he'd made a good choice of getaway vehicle because no one would think to look for missing cows in a bus. He was wrong.

19 December

1992

According to the Hickory *Daily Herald*, Ken Charles Barger was tonight disturbed by the ringing of his telephone. Still more than half-asleep, he reached for the phone (which he kept by his bed) but accidentally picked up his loaded Smith and Wesson .38 special instead. The gun discharged when he put it to his ear, ensuring that he never did manage to take that call.

20 December

1998

The Christmas party antics of Abigail Saxon, a BBC religious programmes producer, didn't just become the talk of her office – they earned her a mention in no less an organ than the *Daily Telegraph*. Saxon, who worked on Radio 4's *Sunday* programme, was mentioned by name in the august journal, which said she was facing disciplinary action 'after running three times around a trendy restaurant bar wearing only her socks'.

She is reported to have twice toured naked around Manchester's upmarket Barca restaurant during an office Christmas lunch, allegedly for a £100 bet. Having collected her winnings, she then completed a third turn, with a cry of 'this one is for free!'

Her colleagues were said to be stunned when she accepted the challenge – and no doubt delighted when she dashed off to the lavatory, removed all of her clothes (apart from her socks), stuck one leg out of the door and shouted, 'Here I come!'

Speaking after the event, a BBC spokesperson said, 'The BBC would not under any circumstances condone such behaviour'. Fortunately, the sporting Ms Saxon kept her job.

21 December

1992

A gust of wind caused a plane to crash just outside the resort town of Faro in Portugal. Two hundred and eighty of the 340 passengers survived, among them Wim Kodman, a botanist. Kodman later said that the turbulence had already sent his friend into a panic before the plane began to go down and that he had made an unsuccessful attempt to calm him. 'I told him, "I'm a scientist – we're objective",' he said. 'I told him a crash was improbable. I was trying to remember the exact probability when we smashed into the ground.'

22 December

2005

According to his former owner, Chris Taylor, Ziggy the African grey parrot was a better mimic than professional comedians. He could accurately imitate Chris's friends, as well as voices from television and radio, and his repertoire even extended to convincing interpretations of the doorbell, microwave and alarm clock. But the bird's very best impression was of Chris's girlfriend, Suzy, whom he was able to render with remarkable accuracy.

Every time her mobile phone rang, for instance, the parrot would squawk out 'Hiya Gary' in an exact take-off of Suzy's Leeds accent, much to his doting owner's amusement. Chris also said he found it funny that the parrot made kissing noises whenever the name Gary was mentioned on the TV. It was only when he was cuddling Suzy on the sofa and Ziggy blurted out 'I love you Gary' in Suzy's voice that the penny finally dropped.

'It sent a chill down my spine', Chris said later. 'I started laughing, but when I looked at Suzy I could tell something was up. Her face was like beetroot, and she started to cry.' She then confessed to a month-long affair with someone called Gary, who visited her at home while Chris was out at work but Ziggy was still on his perch.

The relationship ended that very night, and the couple spent Christmas apart. Sadder still for Chris, however, was the fact that he also had to get rid of his beloved Ziggy since he was unable to teach him not to keep repeating the name of the man who had stolen his woman.

'I wasn't sorry to see the back of Suzy after what she did, but it really broke my heart to let Ziggy go', he told reporters after he parted with the parrot. 'I love him to bits, and I really miss having him around, but it was torture hearing him repeat that name over and over again.

23 December

2000

Welshman Ray John intended to spend a peaceful, alcohol-free Christmas. To that end he decided to hide himself away on remote

Caldey Island, off the coast of his native country, among a community of monks who took a twelve-hour vow of silence each night. The only flaw in his plan was that he smuggled in a supply of hooch and, after a festive drink or two, decided to regale the monastery with a few of his favourite carols.

'He was up all night making a terrible racket', Abbot Father Daniel von Santvoort later told intrigued journalists. 'We observe a vow of silence, but it wasn't a very silent night – even if it was Christmas. We couldn't tell him to hush, so I'm afraid some of us had very little peace that night. All we could do was lie in our beds and cover our ears.'

John was asked to leave the island the next day but continued to drink on the mainland, where police found him collapsed on a railway line. Local magistrates fined him £50 for being drunk and disorderly. The saintly monks said that he would be welcome to come to their island again – provided he left his booze at home.

24 December

1996

Richard Gardener discovered that the gun he was using to hammer in Christmas decorations was loaded when he shot himself in the hand. The young man's annoyance was only increased when the bullet continued on and hit his wife in the stomach.

1888

Vincent Van Gogh, annoyed at his failure to wound Paul Gauguin with a razor during an argument in his fellow artist's kitchen, returned to his own home and chopped off his own ear.

25 December

1994

When he spotted an antelope on the side of the road, Nigerian bus driver Niyi Owoeye did the natural thing: he swerved into its way and ran it over. It was only when he went down to retrieve his free meal that he discovered that his victim wasn't an antelope at all but Mr Ratimi Alesanmi, a member of the local Commission for Road Safety.

1888

The artist Vincent Van Gogh arrived at a Paris brothel with a gift for a prostitute whose name history remembers only as Rachel. 'Keep it and treasure it', he told her as he handed over the present. It was his severed ear.

1646

All Christmas dinners of more than three courses were banned by Cromwell's parliament. Also off the menu were mince pies and Christmas pudding, because they were 'abominable and idolatrous'.

26 December

2006

The airport in Denver, Colorado, was thrown into chaos over Christmas 2006. Snowstorms forced the airport to close for more than forty-five hours in what should have been one of its busiest periods, leaving thousands of passengers stranded and keeping them from their families during the festive period.

For the angry passengers this was an especially bitter pill to swallow because such grandiose claims had previously been made about Denver being an 'all-weather' airport. The airport spokesman Chuck Cannon well understood their frustration. On Boxing Day he even told reporters who mentioned the airport's vaunted 'all-weather' status, 'I would like to choke the person who came up with that term'.

Diligent reporters from Associated Press had soon found the offending quote. Denver, someone had said in 1992, is 'the world's first all-weather airport. We will be able to operate as well in a blizzard as Stapleton can on a sunny day.' But who was the guilty person? Step forward Chuck Cannon.

27 December

1814

Joanna Southcott was one of the eighteenth century's most famous and enterprising prophets. Her apocalyptic, anti-Semitic books were unfailingly popular (all sixty of them); she regularly drew huge crowds to meetings, where she would make dramatic predictions and fall into alarming fits, and her habit of publicly berating officials and churchmen ensured that she was never long out of the press.

Her fame reached its height in 1814, her sixty-fifth year, when she announced that, even though she was still a virgin, she was pregnant – with the next Messiah, whom she planned to name Shiloh. This claim was proved wrong, when she died on 27 December of the same year.

Post-mortems revealed that, rather than a bouncing baby Son of God, she'd been carrying around an ugly cancerous growth. Her large band of followers didn't despair, however, because just before her death Southcott did manage to bequeath them a large sealed box, which she said contained no less than the prophecy of the millennium as foretold in the gospel of St John and the secret to eternal bliss.

The box came with the instructions that it wasn't to be opened until a time of great crisis – and only then in the presence of no fewer than twenty-four bishops of the Church of England. That didn't stop the antiquarian researcher Harry Price taking a look in 1927, when he staged a public opening, together with only one (rather reluctant) prelate, the Bishop of Grantham. Price and his onlookers were surprised to find that rather than eternal bliss, the box contained a horse pistol, a lottery ticket, a dice box, a purse, some old books and, most enigmatically of all, a nightcap.

28 December

1980

Early on this Sunday morning residents on Stratford Road, near Birmingham, were surprised to see an excavator and demolition team speeding past their houses. Unusual as this sight was on the Sabbath, however, the real surprise came in the fact that the contractors drove right past the dilapidated and dangerous cow sheds that they had been asked to destroy and turned off on the wrong side of the road towards Monkspath Hall, an eighteenth-century listed building and one of the most famous farmhouses in the West Midlands. A bigger shock was still to come when the zealous team started to tear lovely Monkspath Hall down. They were so efficient that they finished their work within forty-five minutes, long before any official could be summoned to inform them of their mistake.

29 December

2006

In September 2006 the State University at Kennesa, Georgia, USA unveiled its new $1 million sculpture. It was called *Spaceship Earth* and was described by its Finnish sculptor, 'Eino', as a symbol of how precious our planet is. The main part of the artwork was a 175-ton replica of the earth, 15 feet wide, made of 88 blocks of dark blue, hard-wearing Brazilian quartzite stone. On top of this great mass sat a bronze figure of the pioneering environmentalist David Brower, and sealed inside the structure, which was held together with industrial glue, there was a time capsule that was supposed to remain unseen for the next millennium.

Late in the evening today, campus police felt the floor shake in their office. They rushed outside to see that *Spaceship Earth* had crashed to the ground and disintegrated. All that was left was a pile of rubble and twisted metal and the time capsule, exposed to the elements a good 999.8 years too early. The engraved phrase 'our fragile Earth' was still visible among the debris.

'Kind of ironic', said a university employee with a firm grasp of the basics of the situation.

30 December

1999

Today Trevor Tasker finally got a picture of the woman he had been fervently courting on the web for several months. And it was a corker. 'Wow!' was how Trevor described the shot of a scantily clad beauty with arms teasingly drawn across her front to hide her ample breasts. 'She looked great!'

It was this photo that finally made up 28-year-old Trevor's mind. He was going to make the long journey from his home in north Yorkshire in England to steamy South Carolina in the USA, where he was going to be with the woman he loved, Wynema Shumate.

Shortly after the turn of the millennium, when he arrived in America to start his new life, he received a nasty shock. Waiting for him at the airport, instead of a svelte young stunner, there stood a grey-haired, 20-stone, 65-year-old. Wynema admitted that the picture she had sent him was actually more than thirty years out of date.

In spite of this disappointment, Trevor agreed to go back home with Wynema. Shortly after they arrived, things got even worse for the poor Yorkshireman. The police came round. They wanted to know why money was still being paid to Wynema from the account of her employer, Jim O'Neil, even though he had been registered missing for several months. Wynema suddenly started to look very scared.

'Jim is in the freezer on ice', she blurted. 'I didn't kill him, but I panicked when he died because I'd be without a home and I've got nothing to live for . . . I used a rusty axe. He didn't fit in the freezer, so I tried to chop his leg off.'

Sure enough, police found a corpse in the freezer. An autopsy revealed that O'Neil had died of natural causes, but Wynema was sent to jail on charges relating to fraud and abusing a corpse. Trevor returned home, older and wiser. 'I'll never log on again', he said.

31 December

1929

The secretary of the US Treasury, Andrew G. Mellon, had reassuring words for the world: 'I see nothing in the present situation that is either menacing or warrants pessimism . . . I have every confidence that there will be a revival of activity in the spring, and that during this coming year the country will make steady progress.'

1899

Equally wrong was the commissioner of the US patent office Charles Duell's assessment for the end of the nineteenth century: 'Everything that can be invented has been invented.'

1750

Benjamin Beckonfield, otherwise known as Ben the coal-heaver, was hanged for stealing a hat worth 5 shillings.

Acknowledgements

Susan Smith and Rowan Yapp for invaluable agenting and editing. For sending me ideas and stories and for general moral support: Eloise Millar, Ed Baines, Diana Jordison, David Jordison, Jean Jordison, Luke Williams, Robin Dietch, Paul Day, Thomas Raleigh, David Ridings, Girpis Dowling. Thanks also to the nice people at San Jose public library for confirming the Martin Luther King story.

I've used, abused and plundered so many books, websites and primary sources in order to create *Annus Horribilis* that it would be impossible to list them all here. I would, however, like to acknowledge a particular debt of gratitude to the excellent website snopes.com, an invaluable source of information and a great way of ensuring that – to the best of my knowledge – I've avoided including any urban legends in these pages.

If you've enjoyed this book, I'd also highly recommend *Brewer's Rogues, Villains and Eccentrics*, by William Donaldson. Similarly, Stephen Pile's *Book of Heroic Failures* only gets funnier over time, and R. Chambers's *Book of Days* is a wonderful treasure trove of bizarre information (available online at the time of writing at: http://www.thebookofdays.com/).

Index